*How to Think About
the American Revolution*

Other Books by Harry V. Jaffa

Author

Thomism and Aristotelianism: A Study of the Commentary by Thomas Aquinas on the Nicomachean Ethics (University of Chicago Press, 1952; Reprinted, Greenwood Press, 1979).

Crisis of the House Divided: An Interpretation of the Issues in the Lincoln–Douglas Debates (Doubleday, 1959; Reissued in Paper, with a new Introduction, University of Washington Press, 1973).

Equality and Liberty: Theory and Practice in American Politics (Oxford University Press, 1965).

The Conditions of Freedom: Essays in Political Philosophy (The Johns Hopkins University Press, 1975).

Contributing Author

History of Political Philosophy, Edited by Leo Strauss and Joseph Cropsey (Rand McNally, 2nd ed., 1972).

Shakespeare's Politics, by Allan Bloom, with H.V.J. (Basic Books, 1964).

Editor

In the Name of the People: Speeches and Writings of Lincoln and Douglas in the Ohio Campaign of 1859, with Robert W. Johannsen (Ohio State University Press, 1959).

How to Think About the American Revolution

A Bicentennial Cerebration

HARRY V. JAFFA

Carolina Academic Press
Durham, North Carolina

Printed in the United States of America

Carolina Academic Press
P.O. Box 8791, Forest Hills Station
Durham, North Carolina   27707

To
Carleton and Eileen Appleby

Contents

Preface

How to Think About the American Revolution is a bicentennial "cerebration" intended to mark a milestone in my attempt, now of more than thirty years duration, to understand the American political tradition as it has understood itself. That attempt was recorded at length in *Crisis of the House Divided* (1959), an interpretation of the issues in the Lincoln–Douglas Debates. In it I set forth Lincoln's thesis that the principle of equality, as embodied in the Declaration of Independence, was the central idea from which all the minor thoughts of the American political tradition had radiated. This thesis was further elaborated in *Equality and Liberty* (1965), in which I argued that the Civil War was "the most characteristic phenomenon in American politics, not because it represents a statistical frequency, but because it represents the innermost character of that politics." I have elaborated this thesis in still other ways in *The Conditions of Freedom* (1975).

In the present volume, I pursue further the method followed in *Crisis*, of showing the contemporary academic debate concerning the meaning of the American political tradition as itself a form of the political debate within that tradition. In short, I argue that the "academic" debate is not strictly speaking academic at all. I take up the argument of the late Professor Willmoore Kendall, that Abraham Lincoln had "derailed" the American political tradition, by attributing to the Declaration of Independence, and to the principle of equality, an importance they had never had in the formative years of the Founding. In arguing against Kendall's assertion I have presented evidence that it is little if anything more than a variation of arguments advanced by John C. Calhoun in 1848. The only difference between Kendall and Calhoun appears to be that the latter had held Jefferson responsible for the "derailment" Kendall later attributed to Lincoln. I have argued further that Professors Irving Kristol, and the late Martin Diamond, in notable and highly influential bicentennial addresses adopt in varying ways the same underlying Calhoun thesis. In this way it appears to me that the issues of the Civil War still dominate the question of the inner meaning of the American regime and of the nature of the American experiment in free government.

I believe I have elaborated for the first time the full range of the teaching of the Declaration of Independence. I maintain that its political teaching is more radically democratic than has hitherto been understood. At the same time, I have tried to show how that democratic teaching is subject to implementation by a subtle understanding of the dictates of prudence. Still more, I have maintained that the democracy of the Declaration is shaped and informed at every point by its constitutionalism. The sovereignty of the people can be expressed only in conjunction with the rule of law and never apart from it.

The principle of equality is not merely an assertion about man, but about man, God, and the universe. The heart of the Declaration is a natural theology, something no longer even considered by the *savants* of the contemporary academy. But the relationship of the Creator and of the God of the laws of nature both expresses and justifies the ground of the authority of the people. This teaching of the Declaration, I maintain, remains a model of reasonableness, superior in its understanding of the just powers of government to every attempt to supersede it that has been made in the intervening two hundred years. Nothing threatens the future of human freedom more than the failure to keep alive the understanding of, and attachment to its principles.

LEO STRAUSS IS THE MAN who in our time has made possible the serious study of political philosophy.* He is therefore the one who has made possible the serious study of the Declaration of Independence and of the regime founded upon its teaching. For the Declaration—as we have noted—expresses the conviction that there is a permanent order in the universe by which human beings ought, directly or indirectly, to be guided, whether as men or as citizens.

---

*See "Leo Strauss: 1899–1973," in *The Conditions of Freedom*. The Johns Hopkins University Press, 1975.

This conviction—the heart of the Declaration—is also the one upon which the idea of natural right—the idea of political philosophy—stands or falls. In the two centuries which have followed the Declaration the idea of natural right has been supplanted in the West—for the most part—by the idea of history. The authoritative account of this supplanting is to be found in Strauss's writings, notably in *Natural Right and History* (1953). Hence I see the defense of the serious study of political philosophy—and therewith the defense of the serious study of the Declaration of Independence—to coincide in the defense of the serious study of the writings of Leo Strauss. For this reason, I have added an Appendix on "Political Philosophy and Honor," which embodies such a defense. For surely the misunderstanding of Strauss's philosophic mission—however inadvertent—by those who are thought to represent that mission, is a more serious matter than any of the attacks upon it by its avowed enemies.

Acknowledgments

"Equality as a Conservative Principle" is reprinted with the kind permission of the publisher, from Loyola of Los Angeles Law Review, Vol. 8, June 1975, No. 2., pp. 471–505. "Equality, Justice, and the American Revolution" and "Political Philosophy and Honor" are reprinted with the kind permission of the publisher, from *Modern Age*, Vol. 21, Number 2 (Spring 1977), pp. 114–126, and Vol. 21, Number 4 (Fall 1977), pp. 387–394.

I wish to express my particular appreciation to the American Enterprise Institute for permission to quote *ad libitum* from *America's Continuing Revolution* (Anchor Books, 1976).

I. Introduction: July 4, 1976

WE CELEBRATE TWO HUNDRED YEARS of American independence. We turn as ever upon this day, to the document which declared that independence. Yet we do so, I fear, more in the spirit of those who look wistfully to the past, than of those who look confidently to the future. ("Oh, to be eighty again!" exclaimed ninety year old Justice Oliver Wendell Holmes, Jr., as he spied a pretty girl, while walking in Rock Creek Park on a spring day.)

In 1776 the United States was so to speak nothing; but it promised to become everything. In 1976, the United States, having in a sense become everything, promises to become nothing. It is the central theme of these essays, that the American Revolution is not to be identified primarily with events of the past, but that it is essentially an idea: an idea of political freedom. It is an idea whose successes in the years immediately following the Founding, prompted Abraham Lincoln to say, in 1838, that

> We find ourselves under the government of a system of political institutions, conducing more essentially to the ends of civil and religious liberty, than any of which the history of former times tells us.

Of course, the study of such an idea requires that we contemplate the events in which it is manifested. It is to be found in the story of the birth and growth of the polity. It is to be found in those crises— above all, the Civil War—in which the life principle of that polity was challenged, and its life threatened. But it should also be sought in the way in which the citizens of the republic have shaped their lives to reflect a principle, and shaped their polity to reflect themselves. A "philosophical cause" may be traced in its effects, but it is never exhausted by them. What is inherently true or just is in itself timeless. And so Abraham Lincoln, in 1859, wrote as follows.

> All this is not the result of accident. It has a philosophical cause. Without the *Constitution* and the *Union*, we could not have attained the result; but even these, are not the primary cause of our great prosperity. There is something

1

back of these, entwining itself more closely about the human heart. That something, is the principle of "Liberty to all"—the principle that clears the *path* to all—gives *hope* to all—and, by consequence, *enterprize*, and *industry* to all.

The expression of that principle, in our Declaration of Independence, was most happy, and fortunate. *Without* this, as well as *with* it, we could have declared our independence of Great Britain; but *without* it, we could not, I think, have secured our free government, and consequent prosperity. [All emphasis is in the original]

Today no one would contend that the principle, or principles, of the Declaration entwine themselves about the hearts of the citizens of this republic. How would it be possible to do so, when those principles are hardly understood? At best such principles are thought of as curiosities of a quaint past—where George Washington slept, as distinct from what he was when awake!

The explanation of the decline of the principles of the Declaration of Independence, in the minds and hearts of Americans, is part of a larger story. That is the story of the decline of those principles, both of reason and of revelation, that have formed the core of Western Civilization. From the American perspective, however, I would offer an example of the kind of book which has contributed to this pervasive deterioration. Such a book is, of course, more a symptom than a cause. But it enables us to begin a diagnosis of our condition, to know "where we are, and whither we are tending." *The American Political Tradition, and The Men Who Made It,* by the late Richard Hofstadter, was first published in 1948, but has been reprinted times without number, both in hardcover and paperback editions. A twenty–fifth anniversary edition was brought out in 1973 amid much fanfare. No single work, I think, has done more to change traditional attitudes towards American history in American college classrooms in the last generation.

Such an influence is of course automatically transmitted to the primary and secondary schools. It is a witty and highly readable distillation of much of the debunking scholarship (also called "revisionism") of the previous generation. Much of that scholarship stemmed from a politically conservative (usually either Southern or Border State) attack on Northern anti–slavery Civil War historio-

I. Introduction

graphy. Revisionist scholarship regarded either as ridiculous or mischievous (or both) any attempt to ground American politics upon the "higher law" doctrines ascribed to the Declaration of Independence. Hofstadter's genius was to graft a left–wing political bias upon a right–wing scholarship. His success anticipated in many ways a number of widely read current writers (not a few of them Marxist) who, while not actually defending chattel slavery, compare it not altogether unfavorably with the institutions patronized by slavery's historic critics. That is to say, they gratify the passions of the political right, by their comparative appreciation of the ante–bellum South, and they gratify the political left, by their attack on the institutions of "so–called" free society. Their common ground with Professor Hofstadter—as with the authors against whom these essays are directed—is the depreciation of the principles of the Declaration of Independence.

The *American Political Tradition* is one of those intensely supercilious works that flatters the reader by persuading him that it is telling him all, and even more than all, that he needs to know (without any effort on his part) in order to become an *avant garde* intellectual and critic in the field. To comprehend its popularity and authority, is to understand why American history is rapidly disappearing from the curricula of our public schools. In *Crisis of The House Divided*, published in 1959 (reprinted in paperback, 1973), I had occasion to test the quality of Professor Hofstadter's revisionist historiography. I did so by examining his presentation of the issues in the Lincoln–Douglas debates, which occurs in a chapter entitled "Abraham Lincoln and the Self–Made Myth." In it Hofstadter exerts himself to exhibit Lincoln as a politician who, however shrewd or however eloquent, in the decisive respect was no different, or better, than any other politician. He is at considerable pains to cite the charges made by Douglas against Lincoln during the celebrated Illinois campaign of 1858. He repeats Douglas's assertion that Lincoln was a political trimmer—that is, that he had taken different positions before different audiences—and that these positions were inconsistent with each other. The charge of inconsistency had particular reference to the question of the rights to which Lincoln had asserted Negroes were entitled. Having repeated Douglas's charges, how-

3

ever, Professor Hofstadter utterly fails to report Lincoln's replies. Worse even than that, he fails even to let his readers know that Lincoln *had* made such replies. But the texts of Lincoln's speeches dealing with Douglas's accusations are lengthy and detailed. How they are to be interpreted is a matter requiring not only scholarly accuracy, but philosophical competence. Certainly, a thoughtful student might draw different conclusions from those of Hofstadter, or his revisionist preceptors. One might even come to the conclusions to which I came in *Crisis of the House Divided*, conclusions highly favorable to Lincoln's consistency as a thinker, and to his integrity, both as a politician and a man. Whatever latitude we might rightly concede to differences in interpretation, what can we think of the integrity of a scholar, who repeats the charges of a man's political opponent, made in the heat of a campaign, and then fails to mention the reply to those charges? It was false of Hofstadter to imply that Lincoln had not answered Douglas. But it is true that Hofstadter never, to our knowledge, noticed these charges against his own scholarship, published in 1959 in *Crisis of the House Divided*.

The chapter on the Founding Fathers, with which *The American Political Tradition* begins, ends by declaring that "no man who is as well abreast of modern science as the Fathers were of eighteenth century science believes any longer in an unchanging human nature." But it is Professor Hofstadter's view, no less than it is ours, that the entire political teaching of the Founding Fathers—everything they believed and taught concerning human equality and unalienable rights, concerning balanced and limited government— is grounded in their convictions in regard to nature or, as the Declaration of Independence says, in regard to "the laws of nature and of nature's God." (But consider also the avowal, as a ground of the Constitution, in the 43rd *Federalist*, of a "transcendent law of nature and of nature's God.")

At the end of the same chapter, Professor Hofstadter also writes that "Modern humanistic thinkers who seek for a means by which society may transcend eternal conflict and rigid adherence to property rights as its integrating principles can expect no answer in the philosophy of balanced government as it was set down by the

4

I. Introduction

Constitution-makers of 1787." Yet Professor Hofstadter curiously misrepresents the argument of the famous 10th *Federalist* on the way to this conclusion. Earlier he had written, that "One thing that the Fathers did not propose to do, because they thought it was impossible, was to change the nature of man to conform with a more ideal system." In evidence whereof, he had asserted that according to Madison "the causes of political differences and of the formation of factions were 'sown in the nature of man' and could never be eradicated." Now Madison *had* written that the "latent causes of faction [were] sown in the nature of man." But he was so far from saying that these causes were ineradicable, that he had declared flatly there were *two* methods of removing them. The first of these was by "destroying the liberty which is essential to its existence." The second was by "giving to every citizen the same opinions, the same passions, and the same interests." The first method corresponds to the despotism denounced in the Declaration of Independence. The second apparently corresponded to that of the anti–Federalist advocates of small republics, whom Madison characterizes as "theoretic politicians." These seem to have been doctrinaires of a kind of utopian agrarianism, in which faction was overcome by something akin to Rousseau's general will (by which, we recall, men might be "forced to be free"). Such an alternative seemed no more expedient or desirable to Madison than it would to us, and he accordingly dismissed it. Yet the fact remains, that Madison did not regard as *impossible*,* the project of giving to everyone the same opinions, passions, and interests. Nor did he, contrary to Hofstadter, think it would require any change in human nature to accomplish it. He objected to it, as we object to it, as inconsistent with the idea of a free society. Madison was familiar with the authoritarian societies of

---

*It is true that, having declared that there are "two methods of removing the causes of faction," in the fourth paragraph of the tenth *Federalist*, he says in the tenth paragraph that "The inference to which we are brought is, that the *causes* of faction cannot be removed, and that relief is only to be sought in the means of controlling its *effects*." But this latter assertion—as is clear from the context—means that there is no way of removing the causes of faction *if* we are unwilling—as Madison is unwilling—to make sure use of either of the two methods previously mentioned.

the past, as we are with the totalitarian societies of the present. The uniformity and conformity demanded by such regimes was, and is, the rule rather than the exception in human experience.

What then did Professor Hofstadter mean by that modern "humanism" that would teach us to "transcend eternal conflict and rigid adherence to property rights," by transcending the archaic constitutionalism of the Founding Fathers? What can be meant by his suggesting that we rid our politics of the evils of faction, not by controlling its effects, but by "chang[ing] the nature of man to conform with a more ideal system?" Since we are never explicitly told—although apparently expected to know—we can only speculate. We do know that about the time *The American Political Tradition* was being written, there flourished a species of "humanism" called Stalinism. Loudly trumpeted was the doctrine of a so-called geneticist named Lysenko, which preached "the unity of the organism with its environment," and denied that there were any genetic factors of organisms which could not ultimately be altered by alterations in the environment. Whatever the fate of Stalin's proteges, this has remained the core of official Marxist–Leninist teaching, in opposition to "bourgeois" science, whether social or natural. Notably, it is the response to the social science of James Madison, and to his judgment concerning the possibility and desirability of factionless society. By this Marxist–Leninist teaching, private property is not a reflection of human nature; on the contrary, what is called human nature is only a reflection of private property. Hence to abolish private property is to abolish the "nature" which it has generated. From this point of view—which certainly appears to have been Hofstadter's point of view—there are no intrinsic obstacles in nature to realizing "a more ideal system." And that is why the constitutionalism of the Fathers is said to be obsolete.

Professor Irving Kristol has gained something of a national reputation in recent years as a spokesman for American conservatism. No one, it would seem, could be more orthodox in his regard for the wisdom of the Founding Fathers. In a widely publicised essay on "American Historians and the Democratic Idea," first published in *The American Scholar* (Winter, 1969–1970), and reprinted in *On the Democratic*

6

I. Introduction

Idea in America (New York: Harper & Row, 1972), Professor Kristol takes the historical profession to task for failing to explain how the thoughtful and sophisticated "democratic political philosophy" of the Founding Fathers could have been transformed into the crude "democratic faith" of later times. According to Professor Kristol, the Fathers saw popular government—to which they were profoundly committed—not as an object of faith, but as a problem to be solved. They saw its success as doubtful, and they thought its attainment required the greatest refinement of political wisdom. They were at the opposite extreme from those who see the disorders of democracy as due to anything except the intrinsic difficulties of popular government itself, and who declaim that the only cure for the ills of democracy, is more democracy! According to Professor Kristol, the political teaching of the Fathers is of the greatest relevance to us; according to Professor Hofstadter, that teaching is almost totally irrelevant. No opposition of viewpoints would seem, on the face of it, to be more complete. Hence it should be surprising, if not astonishing, to find that when Professor Kristol declares who it is, among the historians of his own lifetime, whom he finds "most instructive and most 'relevant'," the first name he mentions is that of Professor Hofstadter!

The paradox will, we think, be considerably attenuated for anyone who reads our critique of Professor Kristol's bicentennial lecture, which forms the first part of the title essay of this volume. There he will find that, contrary to what one might expect from the essay in *The American Scholar*, Professor Kristol's praise of the Founding Fathers, or of the political doctrines of the Revolution, is severely limited. It seems to apply to something that might be called the Fathers' "practice" as distinct from their "theory." The latter Kristol describes from time to time as "rhetoric," and counsels us not to take it too seriously. Professor Hofstadter, on the other hand, saw the Fathers' constitutional doctrines and their conception of human nature as essentially in harmony with each other, or as forming a genuine whole. Of course, it was a whole he rejected. Still, in his perception of its integrity—an integrity which it is a major concern of this volume to articulate and to maintain—we believe he was much sounder than Professor Kristol.

Had Professor Kristol attended more closely to Hofstadter's reason for rejecting the political teachings of the Founding Fathers, he would have found the key to the answer to his own question, of why their "political philosophy" should have been replaced by a "political faith." For that key is to be found precisely in Hofstadter's assertion that modern science had rendered unbelievable the idea of an "unchanging human nature." It is to be found, not merely in the assertion itself, but in the certainty with which we find it pronounced. This certainty is such that Hofstadter found it unnecessary to support it by a word of argument or of evidence, or even by reference to the place or places where such argument or evidence might be found. Here we are in the presence of a massive public dogma, for which as little need of proof is felt, as is to be supposed of any Papal prouncement *ex cathedra* in thirteenth century Rome. However, the idea that scientific progress had caused the political teachings of the Revolution to be superseded is not new. Those who read on to the last essay in this volume, will find in the passages of Alexander Stephens "corner stone" speech of 1861, an official defense of the Confederacy, and an official claim of the superiority of the Confederate Constitution to the United States Constitution, based upon the same alleged ground of scientific progress. Yet we believe it to be true, and it is the central thesis of this book—which we invite anyone to controvert—that the evidence for the central doctrines of the Revolution has not changed one iota in the last two hundred years. Whatever might have been said in their favor then might be said now; whatever might be said against them now, might have been said then. Nor do we believe that the state of the case is susceptible to change in the future.

We would here enter a cavil against Professor Hofstadter's expression, "unchanging . . . nature." However rhetorically apt, it is nevertheless logically redundant. For the idea of nature is itself the idea of an unchanging ground of changing phenomena. If it is true, for example that "all men are created equal," then it is true that it is true everywhere and always. To this we would add the thesis, drawn from Leo Strauss's *Natural Right and History* (University of Chicago Press, 1953), that philosophy itself was born in the discovery of nature, and political philosophy in the discovery of man's political nature. (Professor Kristol incidentally mentions Leo

I. Introduction

Strauss as one of the two contemporaries who have done most to "shape [his] thought.") According to *Natural Right and History* the attempt was made some time in the late eighteenth or early nineteenth century, to replace nature with history, as the ground of political philosophy. It is the argument of Strauss's book—an argument widely ignored but, we believe, never refuted—that the end result of that attempt was absolute and unqualified failure. The attempt to replace natural right with historical right ended not in historical political philosophy, but in nihilism. With the abandonment of nature as their ground, the subjects of political philosophy have been transformed—naturally, we are tempted to say—into objects of faith. Given the passion engendered by political attachments, they have been transformed into objects of passionate faith, illuminated (but not tempered) only by the knowledge that there can be no knowledge, either of their ground or of their justification. The question asked by Professor Kristol of what happened to the "democratic political philosophy" of the Founding Fathers is then only a special case of a larger question, of what has happened to political philosophy altogether in the western world. But the break with the tradition of the Fathers, within the American political tradition, can only be studied in conjunction with the break brought on by the defense of slavery, and by the Civil War. Yet this chapter of American history, in which alone the detailed answer to his question can be found, Kristol strangely and studiously ignores. More generally, this inability—exemplified by Professor Kristol—to come to terms, historically or philosophically, with the disruption of the American political tradition occasioned by slavery and scientistic historicism, accounts for the intellectual sterility and political irrelevance of much of so–called present–day American Conservatism. It is symptomatic of its underlying agreement with the Liberalism it purports to attack. For how, in the last analysis, does an unprincipled commitment to the past differ from an unprincipled commitment to the future?

AN APOLOGY, or at least an explanation, is in order, concerning the style of these essays. It is deliberately polemical, and as such intended to remind the reader of the political tradition it evokes. Such a style is distinctly unacademic. Academic disputation today has

9

been aptly characterized by a prominent scholar who remarked that the proper way to refute someone is to ignore him. Certainly that was the mode exemplified by Professor Hofstadter in the case to which we have adverted. It is a mode appropriate to those who believe that the foundations of reason are laid in unreason, and that nothing can ever be concluded, concerning the noble and the base, or concerning the just and the unjust. But we hold with that ancient maxim, that in the refutation of error lies the discovery of truth. Although ours is a regime properly ruled by public opinion, we do not believe that the justice of such a regime ought itself to be a matter of mere opinion.

The issues which trouble this nation as it enters its third century, are not academic, and they cannot be ignored. Paramount is the question of whether the nation was ever destined to be the exemplar of, and witness to, enduring principles. We were not raised to eminence by men who refused confrontation, either in the forum, or on the battlefield. Nor can we long preserve this eminence, except by the means that raised us to it. The great political speeches of American history, in particular those of the first fourscore and seven years, may be compared to their honor with the best of comparable epochs in the history of the Greeks, or of the Romans, or of the English. Nearly all of those speeches (or attendant writings) are political debates, or are the causes or consequences of political debates. It is astonishing that, in the presence of such a rich legacy Professor Kristol, in inaugurating a bicentennial lecture series, should declare that the American political tradition, after the Revolution, became "an inarticulate tradition!"

Professor Kristol makes many and favorable references to *The Federalist* as a book of political philosophy or theory of a high order, and complains that no adequate study of it has yet been made. Yet he fails to see at least one of the most important reasons for this deficiency. For *The Federalist*, however excellent in itself, remains a partisan piece in the bitter political struggle over the ratification of the Constitution. By this we do not suggest that *The Federalist*, being partisan, is defective. We do say, however, that the character of its partisanship is not fully visible, except in the light of the arguments advanced on the other side. With the forthcoming work on the Anti-Federalists by Professor Herbert Storing of the University of Chicago, this obstacle should be removed.

If, as Professor Kristol rightly declares, *The Federalist* is praiseworthy because it regards democracy or popular government as problematic, this is immeasurably more true of a later work. Of *The Political Debates of Abraham Lincoln and Stephen A. Douglas*, published by Follett, Foster and Company, Columbus, Ohio in the spring of 1860, we may say that it provides a kind of dialectical epitome of nearly a half-century of political conflict, concerning the question which, far more than any other in its history, has divided the American people. As a single work it has the advantage of having a partisan of either side to present his case, not only to an audience, but directly to each other. It is such a book as Publius might have produced, had Brutus or Cato been asked (and agreed) to write every second number.

But the interest of the Lincoln–Douglas debates stems less from the accident of its form, than from the essential importance of its subject-matter, and from the depth and power of the arguments of either side. The question of whether or how slavery should be admitted or excluded from federal territory in the 1850s, involved consideration of whether and why slavery itself was just or unjust. That is to say, it involved consideration of the intrinsic differences, and intrinsic merits, of despotic government (slavery) and constitutional government (freedom). This in turn involved the question of whether, and in what way the principle of popular government was majority rule. It raised the question of how consent became the legitimating principle of free government. Nowhere in American political literature—certainly not in *The Federalist*—is the rule of the people, considered merely as the rule of the many, more severely challenged or debated. In the Peoria speech of 1854, Lincoln had quoted this paraphrase by Douglas of the free–soil argument. "The white people of Nebraska are good enough to govern themselves, *but they are not good enough to govern a few miserable negroes!!*" To this Lincoln replied, "Well, I doubt not that the people of Nebraska are, and will continue to be as good as the average of people elsewhere. I do not say the contrary. What I do say is, that no man is good enough to govern another man, *without that other's consent.*"

11

The debate between Lincoln and Douglas raised, or re-raised, the question of the meaning of the principles of the Revolution, perhaps more profoundly than they had been considered in the Revolution itself. For it sought the *enduring* meaning of those principles in the *changing* circumstances of more than two generations. Moreover, it sought the meaning of those principles, not to discover what the American people might demand *for* themselves before the rest of the world. It sought to discover what, in the light of those principles, might be demanded by the American people, *of* themselves. It sought to define such demands, not for their approval by a candid world, but for their approval by that less visible but more demanding forum, their own consciences. Accordingly, it raised the question of what kind of a people a free people ought to be, to justify what was now seen not merely to be a right, but an inestimable privilege, the privilege of being governed freely by their own consent. The American Revolution may have begun on the battlefields of Lexington and Concord, but its true climax came upon the battlefield of Gettysburg.

Let us then look soberly to our third century. This hour, as many that have gone before it, is piled high with difficulty. Yet we may face the future with a goodly inheritance, if we will possess ourselves of what is rightly ours. Shall we go naked to our enemies, while our ancient faith, like ancient armor, rusts in monumental mockery? That "abstract truth, applicable to all men and all times," that "rebuke and stumbling block. . .to tyranny and oppression," that Lincoln found in the Declaration of Independence, is still there. But how can we be made to see that it is still there, when we are always told to look the other way?

II. Equality as a Conservative Principle*

So whatever you wish that men would do to you, do so to them; for this is the law and the prophets.

—*Jesus*

As I would not be a *slave*, so I would not be a *master*. This expresses my idea of democracy. Whatever differs from this, to the extent of the difference, is no democracy.

—*Abraham Lincoln*

1.

That Conservatism should search for its meaning implies of course that Conservatism does not have the meaning for which it is searching. This might appear paradoxical, since a Conservative is supposed to have something definite to conserve. Unfriendly critics sometimes suggest that what we Conservatives conserve, or wish to conserve, is money. But since many of us, like Socrates, live in thousand-fold poverty, this is manifestly untrue. Yet our plight might be said to resemble that of a man with a great hoard of gold or diamonds. Suppose such a man suddenly awoke to find that his treasure was no longer precious, and that it held no more meaning for the rest of the world than sand or pebbles. How strange the world would look to that man! How strange that man would look to the world, vainly clinging to his pile of rubbish.

In today's political vocabulary, Conservatism is contrasted with Liberalism and Radicalism. In this strange world, however, I cannot imagine Liberalism or Radicalism searching for meaning. Liberalism and Radicalism are confident of their meaning, and the world is

---

*This essay was originally prepared for delivery at the 1974 annual meeting of the American Political Science Association, at a panel presided over by William F. Buckley, Jr. The theme of the panel was "Conservatism's Search for Meaning."

confident of their confidence. Yet once upon a time, a Liberal was thought to be more diffident. He was someone who recognized the fallibility of human reason and its susceptibility to the power of the passions. He tended therefore to be tolerant of human differences. A liberal regime was one in which such differences were in a sense institutionalized. James Madison's extended republic embracing a multiplicity of factions, in which no faction might become a majority or impose its will upon a majority, is the classic instance in the modern world of such a regime. But the New Liberal is committed to policies which tend not to recognize the propriety of differences. Consider the rigidity of such slogans as "one man, one vote," "racial balance," "affirmative action," "guaranteed income," "war on poverty," "generation of peace." All these imply a degree of certainty as to what is beneficial, which makes those who doubt appear to be obscurantists or obstructionists, standing in the way of welfare either out of stupidity or out of a vested interest in ill fare.

The only significant differences I can see between today's Liberals and today's Radicals concern means rather than ends. How often during the "troubles" of the late 1960s did we hear the Liberals deplore the Radicals' violence, telling them that they should "work within the system"? How often did we hear these same Liberals praise the Radicals for their "idealism," asking only that they learn patience? But the Radicals made a great deal more sense. If their ideals were so praiseworthy, then a system which obstructed their fulfillment was blameworthy. And why work within a blameworthy system for praiseworthy ends?

Liberalism and Radicalism both reject the wisdom of the past, as enshrined in the institutions of the past, or in the morality of the past. They deny legitimacy to laws, governments, or ways of life which accept the ancient evils of mankind, such as poverty, inequality, and war, as necessary—and therefore as permanent—attributes of the human condition. Political excellence can no longer be measured by the degree to which it ameliorates such evils. The only acceptable goal is their abolition. Liberalism and Radicalism look forward to a state of things in which the means of life, and of the good life, are available to all. They must be available in such a way that the full development of each individual—which is how the good life is

14

defined—is not merely compatible with, but is necessary to, the full development of all. Competition between individuals, classes, races, and nations must come to an end. Competition itself is seen as the root of the evils mankind must escape. The good society must be characterized only by cooperation and harmony. The Old Liberalism saw life as a race, in which justice demanded for everyone only a fair or equal chance in the competition. But the New Liberalism sees the race itself as wrong. In every race there can be but one winner, and there must be many losers. Thus the Old Liberalism preserved the inequality of the Few over and against the Many. It demanded the removal of artificial or merely conventional inequalities. But it recognized and demanded the fullest scope for natural inequalities. But the New Liberalism denies natural no less than conventional inequalities. In the Heaven of the New Liberalism, as in that of the Old Theology, all will be rewarded equally. The achievement of the good society is itself the only victory. But this victory is not to be one of man over man, but of mankind over the scourges of mankind. No one in it will taste the bitterness of defeat. No one need say, "I am a loser, but I have no right to complain. I had a fair chance." The joys of victory will belong to all. Unlike the treasures of the past, the goods of the future will be possessed by all. They will not be diminished or divided by being common. On the contrary, they will for that very reason increase and intensify. No one will be a miser— or a Conservative.

I have intimated that what is today called Conservatism—the New Conservatism—may in fact be the Old Liberalism. Indeed, it may be the Old Radicalism as well. Leo Strauss used to delight in pointing out that the most conservative or even reactionary organization in the United States was called the Daughters of the American Revolution. Certainly, if American Conservatism has any core of consistency and purpose, it is derived from the American Founding. The uncertainty as to the meaning of American Conservatism is, as we shall see, an uncertainty as to the meaning of the American Founding. But this uncertainty does not arise from any doubt as to the status of the Revolution. So far as I know, there has never been any Benedict Arnold Society of American Patriotism. Nor do American Conservatives meet, either openly or secretly, to toast "the

King (or Queen) across the water." The status of feudalism and monarchy are for American Conservatives exactly what they are for American Liberals or Radicals. Perhaps the best description of the *Ancien Regime* from the American point of view is still that of Mark Twain in *A Connecticut Yankee in King Arthur's Court.*

American Conservatism is then rooted in a Founding which is, in turn, rooted in revolution. Moreover, the American Revolution represented the most radical break with tradition—with the tradition of Europe's feudal past—that the world had seen. It is true that the American revolutionaries saw some precedent for their actions in the Whig Revolution of 1689. But that revolution at least maintained the fiction of a continued and continuous legality. The British Constitution that resulted from the earlier revolution may have had some republican elements. But the American constitutions—state and federal—that resulted from the later revolution had *no* monarchical or aristocratic elements. They were not merely radically republican, but were radically republican in a democratic sense.[1] The sovereignty of the people has never been challenged within the American regime, by Conservatives any more than by Liberals or Radicals.

The regime of the Founders was wholly devoted to what they understood as civil and religious liberty and was in that sense a liberal regime. But the Founders understood themselves to be revolutionaries, and to celebrate the American Founding is therefore to celebrate revolution. However mild or moderate the American Revolution may now appear, as compared with subsequent revolutions in France, Russia, China, Cuba, or elsewhere, it nonetheless embodied the greatest attempt at innovation that human history had recorded. It remains the most radical attempt to establish a regime of liberty that the world has yet seen.

2.

What were the principles of the American Revolution? What are the roots of the American Founding? One would think that after nearly two hundred years this question could be easily answered. Never did men take more pains to justify what they were doing at every step of the way than did the patriots of the Revolution. Never was

16

the fashioning of a plan of government better documented than that hammered out in Philadelphia in the summer of 1787. Never was such a plan more fully debated before adoption than that which came before the several ratifying conventions. Never was an actual regime, as distinct from a hypothetical one, so enshrined in theoretical reasoning as was the constitution of 1787 in the *Federalist Papers*. And yet the matter is unresolved.

Our perplexity that this should be so is less surprising when we reflect that the course of American history for more than "four score and seven years" was one of deep-seated controversy, culminating in one of the bitterest wars of modern times. Until the resort to arms, these conflicts almost always took the form of debates as to the meaning of the Founding. And the Founding documents, and their principal glosses, were invariably cited on both sides in these debates. In more respects than one, American history and Jewish history resembled each other. Mid-century British liberals, like their American counterparts, were also divided. In 1861 Lord Acton wrote an essay entitled *Political Causes of the American Revolution*,[2] in which he expressed no doubt that the Confederacy was fighting for the same principles of independence for which Washington had fought. But Lord Acton's countryman, John Stuart Mill, in another essay written shortly afterwards,[3] was just as sure that Lincoln's government was fighting to preserve these same principles. That the contestants appealed to the same political dogmas—even as they read the same Bible and prayed to the same God—only intensified the struggle. As sectarians of the same faith, they fought each other as only those fight who see their enemies as heretics.

American Conservatism today is still divided, not surprisingly, along lines which have divided Americans since before the Civil War. Sir Winston Churchill once said that the American Civil War was the last great war fought between gentlemen. Certainly Churchill had in mind the patriotism and the gallantry of men like Lee, Jackson, and Davis on the Confederate side, and Lincoln, Grant, and Sherman on the side of the Union. But I think he also had in mind the dignity of the principles that both sides held, and the tragedy inherent in the possibility that these same principles should seem to speak differently to men of equal integrity and devotion.

17

But gentlemanship, like patriotism, is not enough. Not Jefferson Davis or, for that matter, John C. Calhoun—surely one of the most intelligent men who ever lived—saw as deeply into the meaning of the American principles as Abraham Lincoln. And so—to borrow a phrase from the late Willmoore Kendall—let us have no foolishness about both sides being equally right. That the South lost the war on the battlefield does not in the least mean that it lost the argument. From Alexander Stephens to Willmoore Kendall, its champions have lost none of their fervor. So far are they from admitting defeat, that, on the contrary, they repeatedly proclaim victory.

In a recent book entitled *The Basic Symbols of the American Political Tradition**, Kendall, together with George Carey, takes the position that the arch-heretic, the man who "derailed" our tradition, was Abraham Lincoln. According to Kendall and Carey, all the Liberal and Radical demands, which would today transform constitutional into totalitarian government, are imperatives of Equality. And the power of this idea, or the power which the Radicals and Liberals have derived from it, stems from a misinterpretation or misapplication of the Declaration of Independence. According to Kendall and Carey, the Declaration is not the central document of our Founding, nor is it the true source of the symbols of the Founding. Nor does the expression of the doctrine of Equality in the Declaration mean what Abraham Lincoln said it meant, nor what the Liberals and Radicals of today wish it to mean. Nothing in our pre-Revolutionary past, or in the constitution-building period of the Revolutionary generation, justified making Equality the end or goal to be secured by the American regime. Equality as an end became the official principle of the regime only by a retrospective interpretation of "four score and seven years," an interpretation enshrined by Abraham Lincoln at Gettysburg. The Gettysburg Address, say Kendall and Carey, was a rhetorical trick. It made the victory of the Union armies the occasion for an official transformation of our constitutional, Conservative revolutionary past, into a sanction for a Radical–Liberal revolutionary future.

---

*Baton Rouge: Louisiana State University Press. 1970. Pp. xi, 163.

II. Equality as a Conservative Principle

3.

Now we maintain that the truth about these matters is almost the exact opposite of what Kendall and Carey say it is. We believe that the Declaration of Independence is the central document of our political tradition, not because of any trick played by Abraham Lincoln, but because it is the most eloquent, as well as the most succinct, statement of the political teaching of all the great documents of the period. The sentiments of the Declaration are not unique to it. Jefferson was the draftsman of a representative assembly, and his gift lay in finding memorable phrases that articulated the thoughts that everyone wished expressed. The doctrine of Equality, which is indeed the key to all the thoughts in the Declaration, is also to be found in at least seven of the bills of rights accompanying the original state constitutions.[4] It is implied if not expressed in the Declaration of the First Continental Congress (1774) and in the Declaration of the Causes and Necessity of Taking Up Arms (1775). Kendall and Carey believe that the idea of Equality dropped out of sight when the constitution of 1787 came to be written, and that the constitutional morality of the *Federalist Papers* has nothing to do with it. They are dead wrong on both counts. The idea of Equality, as expressed in the Declaration, is the key to the morality of "the laws of nature and of nature's God." It is this natural law which the Constitution—and the regime of which the Constitution is a feature —is designed to implement. The abandonment of the idea of Equality is perforce an abandonment of that morality and that constitutionalism. It is perforce an abandonment of the "ought" for the "is." It would be an abandonment of that higher law tradition which is the heart of that civility—and that Conservatism—which judges men and nations by permanent standards. As we propose to demonstrate, the commitment to Equality in the American political tradition is synonymous with the commitment to those permanent standards. Whoever rejects the one, of necessity rejects the other, and in that rejection opens the way to the relativism and historicism that is the theoretical ground of modern totalitarian regimes.

4.

Basic Symbols is replete with references to the "enormous impact

19

on American scholarship and thinking"[5] of Lincoln's alleged "derailment" of the American political tradition. Yet Kendall and Carey do not provide a single example of that "derailed" scholarship. The central role of Equality in American life and thought was asserted long ago by Alexis de Tocqueville in his *Democracy in America*, written in the 1830s. Lincoln grew up in the Jacksonian America that Tocqueville had observed, and it is hardly surprising that he responded powerfully to what was already the most powerful force in the world in which he moved. That the Gettysburg Address somehow transformed the *ethos* of American life—and of American scholarship—would have required a demonstration that Kendall and Carey nowhere attempt. It would have required an analysis of Lincoln's reasoning on Equality, in its theoretical and practical bearings, pointing out how and why this was a new way of understanding Equality and how this new way had affected others. That is to say, it would have required evidence that Equality was now understood differently because of Lincoln and that the way Equality was now understood differently because of Lincoln and that the way Equality was now understood was not because of an inheritance from pre-Lincolnian egalitarianism, or from that inheritance modified by any of the other countless writers on the subject.

In fact, the only work which has ever attempted a full analysis of the theoretical and practical meaning of Equality in Lincoln's political thought is my *Crisis of the House Divided*.[6] In it I pointed out that American historical scholarship, insofar as it had perceived the impact of Equality upon Lincoln's policies in the 1850s, had thoroughly rejected it. Indeed, in the field of Lincoln scholarship, as distinct from popular writing, *Crisis of the House Divided* was, as far as I know, the first book in the Twentieth Century to take a distinctly favorable view of Lincoln's policies in the 1850s. Since its publication in 1959, Don E. Fehrenbacher's *Prelude to Greatness: Lincoln in the 1850's* (1962), has made a powerful addition to this point of view.

The seven hundred years' providential march of Equality, of which Tocqueville wrote,[7] has certainly continued, as Tocqueville predicted it would. Many of its effects have been bad, as he also predicted. Tocqueville was much influenced in his view of Jacksonian America by the American Whigs he met—by the party of Adams, Clay, and Webster. He never met a young follower of these men named Abraham Lincoln. Yet Lincoln's articulation of the Whig critique of a demagogic egalitarianism, expressed particularly in his Lyceum (1838)[8] and Temperance (1842)[9] speeches, contains remarkable parallels to Tocqueville. Certainly Lincoln and Tocqueville saw the threat to the nation from slavery and racial difference in very similar ways. To impute an indiscriminate egalitarianism to Lincoln, as Kendall and Carey do, is as absurd as to impute it to Tocqueville.

Vaguely imputing Lincolnian effects to American scholarship, *Basic Symbols* nowhere comes to grips with the character of Lincoln's thought. Nor does it ever allude to the articulation of that thought in *Crisis of the House Divided*. This is all the more remarkable, in that Kendall not only had read *Crisis,* but had published a lengthy review of it in *National Review*,[10] which he reprinted in *The Conservative Affirmation*.[11] Had he thought ill of it, we could understand his passing over it later. But in fact he praised it extravagantly. We believe it to be the most generous review ever written about a book with which the reviewer so thoroughly disagreed. We feel obliged to quote it at some length now, not because of the praise, but because of the disagreement. We do so, moreover, because it seems to us to explain a missing link in *Basic Symbols'* polemic against Lincoln. *Basic Symbols* is silent not only about the actual reasoning in Lincoln's thought about Equality, but also about the great subject that occasioned nearly everything Lincoln said and wrote about Equality: slavery. So far as I can recall, the word "slavery" never occurs in *Basic Symbols*. Yet *Basic Symbols* wrestles with Equality on every page—like Jacob wrestling with the Angel of the Lord, we are tempted to say. To do so, without once mentioning slavery, would be like a critique of Hamlet that never mentions the ghost. Fortunately, Kendall does mention slavery in his review of *Crisis of the House Divided* and enables us thereby to form a juster view of what he says about Equality in *Basic Symbols*.

Kendall states, quite correctly, that "The central problem of

Crisis of the House Divided is the status in the American political tradition of the 'all men are created equal' clause of the Declaration of Independence."[12] He adds that

> . . . Jaffa's Lincoln (and Jaffa) sees it as the indispensable presupposition of the entire American political experience; either you accept it as *the* standard which that experience necessarily takes as its point of departure, or you deny the meaning of the entire American experience. As for the status of Abraham Lincoln *vis-à-vis* the Signers and Framers, Jaffa's Lincoln sees the great task of the nineteenth century as that of affirming the cherished accomplishment of the Fathers by *transcending* it. Concretely, this means to construe the equality clause as having an allegedly unavoidable meaning with which it was always pregnant, but which the Fathers apprehended only dimly.[13]

According to Kendall, the question which is "tacit, but present on every page of the book,"[14] is the question

> whether the Civil War was, from the standpoint of natural right and the cause of self-government, the "unnecessary war" of the historians of the past fifty or sixty years, or a war that *had* to be fought in the interest of freedom for all mankind.
>
> Jaffa's answer to the question is that the war did indeed have to be fought—once the South had gone beyond slaveholding . . . to assert the "positive goodness" of slavery, and so to deny the validity of the equality–clause standard as the basic axiom of our political system. . . . And, *within the limits* to which he for sound reasons of strategy confines himself, Jaffa's case for that answer seems to this reviewer as nearly as possible irrefragable.
>
> His readers will, therefore, be well-advised to keep a sharp lookout *for those limits,* lest Jaffa launch them, and with them the nation, upon a political future the very thought of which is hair-raising: a future made up of an endless series of Abraham Lincolns, each persuaded that he is superior in wisdom and virtue to the Fathers, each prepared to insist that those who oppose this or that new application of the equality standard are denying the possibility of self-government, each ultimately willing to plunge America into Civil War rather than concede his point. . . .
>
> The limits I speak of are set by the alternatives that Jaffa steadfastly—plausibly but steadfastly—refuses to consider, namely: that a negotiated solution might have been worked out in terms of compensating the Southerners for their slaves and attempting some sort of radical confrontation of the Negro problem, and that the Southerners were entitled to secede if the issue was to be drawn in Lincoln's terms.[15]

In his concluding paragraph, Kendall declared:

> The idea of natural right is not so easily reducible to the equality clause,

and there are better ways of demonstrating the possibility of self-government than imposing one's own views concerning natural right upon others.[16]

5.

What are those "limits" which Kendall so earnestly warned my readers to beware? We confess to having been completely unaware of them. If they have served any reasons of strategy the reasons are Kendall's, not ours. These limits turn out, upon inspection, to be certain "alternatives" that we are "plausibly but steadfastly" supposed to have refused to consider. But there is a simple explanation why we did not consider them in *Crisis of the House Divided*. That book was an interpretation of the Lincoln-Douglas debates, which we viewed as embracing the principal issues dividing the American people between the Mexican War and the Civil War. The Preface to *Crisis* stated plainly that it was intended as the first of two volumes. The topics Kendall said we had avoided belonged plainly to the second volume, to the period after Lincoln's election in 1860. There was then no strategy behind our alleged refusal other than a chronological division within my subject.

Although that second volume has not yet appeared, there is a survey of the great issues of Lincoln's presidency in my essay, *The Emancipation Proclamation*.[17] In it I faced squarely enough the issues Kendall said I had avoided in *Crisis*. Kendall knew therefore that if the case for Lincoln was, "as nearly as possible irrefragable" within the hypothetical limits he had assigned to it, it was just as irrefragable despite them. He and Carey simply refused to face that argument in *Basic Symbols* and preferred instead to pretend that it did not exist. We shall see why.

6.

What then were the proposals that Kendall said that Jaffa—he really meant Lincoln—had refused to consider, that might justly have prevented the Civil War? First, "that a negotiated solution might have been worked out in terms of compensating the Southerners for their slaves. . . ."[18] Second, that there might have been "some sort of radical confrontation of the Negro problem."[19] And third, that the South should have been allowed "to secede if the issue was to be drawn in Lincoln's terms."[20]

What in the world did Kendall mean by a "negotiated solution"?

Many attempts at compromise were made in the winter of 1860–1861, the most famous of which bore the name of Senator Crittenden of Kentucky. Many long books have been written about these efforts, and we propose to write another one—but not now. Suffice it to say that Lincoln would not consent to any compromise which involved conceding to the South the right to extend slavery into federal territories. However, under existing federal law—*i.e.*, under the Supreme Court's ruling in the case of *Dred Scott*[21]—there was no legal inhibition in 1861 against any slaveowner actually taking slaves into any federal territory open to settlement. Moreover, there was no immediate prospect that that ruling would change. Nor could there be any Republican or anti-slavery majority in either house of Congress, unless the Southern members absented themselves. It was against fears of the *future* that secession took place, and it is hard to know what compromise Kendall wished Lincoln to endorse that presumably would have made him the statesman of Kendallian consensus. Lincoln himself thought that nothing would satisfy the South at that juncture except a complete reversal on the slavery question by the most moderate and conservative of the anti-slavery leaders. They must cease saying slavery is wrong and that it should be restricted to those states where it was now lawful and must say instead that it is right and should be extended to wherever slaveowners could carry it. Did Kendall believe that, in a free society, men could be asked to declare against their deepest convictions?

Kendall speaks of "compensating the Southerners for their slaves."[22] By this I presume he intends some scheme of compensated emancipation. But given the state of parties and of political opinion in 1860–1861, such a proposal is wildly anachronistic. It would resemble a proposal today that *detente* with the Soviet Union be pursued by a plan for buying up the Soviet state industries and returning them to free capitalistic enterprise. Kendall seems not to recognize that the issues which divided Americans on the eve of the Civil War had no direct nor immediate reference to slavery in the states where it existed, but had solely to do with the *extension* of slavery. In his inaugural address, Lincoln said—repeating a passage from an earlier speech—"'I have no purpose, directly or indirectly, to interfere with the institution of slavery in the States where it exists. I believe I have no lawful right to do so, and I have no inclination to do so.'"[23] For more than a generation, John C. Calhoun had drilled the South in the lesson that they must never, never, never, never, by the remotest inference, concede the slightest federal jurisdiction over the domestic institution of slavery. For example, they must not concede federal power over slavery even in the District of Columbia, because it had been carved out of slave states. Nor must they admit the right of Congress to receive abolitionist petitions even for the purpose of rejecting them. Nor must they admit the right even of the federal post to deliver abolitionist literature in the states that outlawed it. While Lincoln certainly did not share these extreme views, he was nonetheless sympathetic with the difficulties of the white South in dealing with what he called the "necessities" of the actual presence of slavery amongst them. It was just because he estimated those necessities so justly that Lincoln would not consider any compromise that carried slavery into lands where it was not already rooted. But to have proposed emancipation in 1860 or 1861, would have been regarded as an act of bad faith. Far from being an instrument of negotiation or compromise, as Kendall seems to think, it would have been a firebrand.

7.

We digress briefly here to consider the actual plans of emancipation that Lincoln put forward at different times in his career—although not in the secession crisis of 1860–1861. We do so, among other reasons, because they demonstrate the absurdity of a myth that Kendall and Carey assiduously promote, that Lincoln was somehow the spiritual father of the New Deal, of the expanded presidency of the twentieth century, and of the welfare state. Lincoln took almost no part in the formulation of what we might call the "domestic legislation" of his presidency. The Republican Party over which he presided sponsored a great deal of new legislation, dealing with a national banking system, promoting a national railroad system, providing homestead legislation, providing the land grants that led to the great system of state universities, and providing new tariffs for the growing manufacturing industries of the North, and so on.

25

Lincoln signed these bills into law as a matter of course. Most of them were basically Whig measures which he had long endorsed. They were the foundation of that ebullient capitalism later called the age of the "robber barons." Lincoln himself was almost wholly occupied with the prosecution of the war. Any expansions of federal authority attributable to Lincoln stemmed from his interpretation of his constitutional duty "that the Laws be faithfully executed" and from his authority, "in Cases of Rebellion or Invasion," as commander-in-chief. These were crisis powers, they were *not* expansions of the commerce clause, of the general welfare clause, or of any of those enumerated powers by which *Congress* has in the twentieth century added to the powers of the presidency. Lincoln did very little, if anything, to expand the powers of the federal government *per se*. What he did under the war powers did *not* set precedents for an expanded peace time role of the presidency in particular, or for the federal government in general. In fact, much of Lincoln's long struggle against the Congressional Radicals was a struggle to keep Congress from assuming powers over persons and property that Lincoln did not believe the federal government possessed. As long as the executive exercised them, as incidents of the war powers, they did not become permanent additions to federal jurisdiction.

Ever since Lincoln had been a Whig Congressman during the Mexican War he had supported the idea of emancipation for the District of Columbia. Although he believed that Congress had full sovereignty over all aspects of slavery in the District, he was opposed to outright abolition. The plan that had his support had these three elements. First, the abolition had to be gradual. (The plan that he proposed during the Civil War would have allowed up to thirty-seven years for its accomplishment.) Second, it had to be authorized, not only by Congress, but also by a majority of the qualified voters of the District. (Does this sound like Kendall's Lincoln, "imposing his own view concerning natural right upon others"?) And third, compensation had to be made to the owners of the slaves emancipated.

When Lincoln came to propose a national plan for emancipation in December, 1862, it possessed all these elements of voluntarism. To insure that this was so, Lincoln insisted that the authorizing legislation be incorporated in a series of constitutional amendments. These amendments would provide that the federal government be enabled to indemnify those states which had voluntarily adopted systems of gradual, compensated emancipation. The federal government would not, under Lincoln's plan, require the states to adopt such plans. But it would facilitate their doing so, by assuming all or most of the financial burden of such plans. But true to his inaugural pledge that the Constitution did not authorize *any* federal jurisdiction over slavery in the *states*, Lincoln required an amendment to the Constitution even to pay money to enable the states to do more conveniently what they might wish to do about slavery. It is worth noting that Lincoln's proposal would not have provided any precedent for the innumerable federal grant-in-aid programs of the twentieth century. By requiring a constitutional amendment to permit the federal government to pay money to the states for one particular specified purpose, Lincoln would not—to repeat—have done anything to expand federal jurisdiction over the domestic institutions or internal commerce of any state.

But why did Lincoln propose any scheme of emancipation during the war? The answer to this is that Lincoln's inaugural pledge could not be maintained in the face of a war it did not contemplate. By September of 1862 Lincoln was convinced that he had to strike at slavery if the war was to be won and the Union preserved. Every slave who deserted his Confederate master weakened the Confederate economy that much. Every white Southerner who had to stay on farm or factory could not take his place in the Confederate firing line. As we have seen, Lincoln did not believe that either he or the Congress possessed any lawful power over slavery in the states, and whatever powers he possessed over enemy contraband did not apply to loyal owners. The terms of the Emancipation Proclamation included a careful enumeration of all those states and parts of states that were in rebellion against the authority of the United States. The Proclamation had no effect in Delaware, Maryland, Kentucky, Missouri, and large parts of Virginia and Louisiana.

Lincoln knew, and told the Congress, that slavery was doomed everywhere in the United States, if it was doomed anywhere. The process of war was breaking up the entire social and police system, upon which the peculiar institution depended. Lincoln's system of emancipation was the only way he knew to prevent loyal slaveholders from ultimately suffering the same fate as disloyal ones. And there is no doubt in my mind that, had Lincoln's plan been adopted, and had Lincoln survived the war, he would have attempted to secure some indemnification for loyal slaveholders behind the Confederate lines. Lincoln always thought of slavery as a national moral responsibility, even if the legal responsibility was limited by state rights. He did not think that a man who had sold a slave had the right to keep his money, while the man who bought him might rightfully have his purchase confiscated. The confiscation of private property during the war troubled Lincoln deeply, for the same reason that slavery troubled him. For what was slavery itself but a denial of the foundation of all property rights, by the confiscation of the right that a man had in himself and in the fruits of his own labor?

We have told the story of the Emancipation Proclamation in our essay of that name.[24] We mention now only that Lincoln failed to secure the passage of his plan through the Congress. His failure stemmed from his inability to persuade the border slave state Congressmen to support it. Although the border slave states had now sealed their fidelity to the Union with their blood, they were as stubborn as their Confederate brethren in refusing any step that might, in their own minds, and however indirectly, admit the wrongfulness of slavery. There was both a guilt and a pride which seems to have infected all who had been immediately touched by the peculiar institution. They would not take the most obvious measures in their own interest, if by so doing they might seem to cast a reproach upon their own past. Kendall and Carey's inability even to mention slavery in a book dominated by that subject testifies that the power of that reproach has not yet ceased. But the thirteenth amendment, necessary as it proved to be, ended the legal existence of slavery in the United States in a way which Lincoln never desired. But the failure to achieve a better way cannot be made a matter of reproach to him.

8.

Among the alternatives that Kendall said that Jaffa—and Lincoln—
had refused to consider was "some sort of radical confrontation of
the Negro problem."[25] But this is just as nebulous as the proposal of
a "negotiated solution" to the sectional crisis. If it means anything,
it means facing the social and political consequences of eventual and
complete emancipation. But of course there had been a great deal of
contemplation of this possibility. And the South had concluded,
because of it, that emancipation must never come. The North had
also concluded, because of it, that slavery must never be extended.
The free state settlers in the territories had no wish to meet Negroes
there, free or slave. And the slave South believed that unless
slavery were to expand, it would eventually contract, and that emancipation would come as an economic, if not as a political, necessity.
And so there was a steady hardening of positions on both sides.

In the decade before the Civil War the laws governing slavery
had grown steadily harsher. It became impossible in many states for
owners to free slaves, even if they wished to do so. Many of the
slaves that such owners wished to free were of course their own
children. There are countless stories—not all of them invented by
Harriet Beecher Stowe—of the deathbed agonies of men whose
children were security for their debts and who would be sold "down
the river" after their demise. Because of fear of this, some wealthy
New Orleans families sent their mulatto children to France. The
laws also became stringent in forbidding teaching slaves to read, in
forbidding their congregating except under strict supervision, in
forbidding association between slaves and free Negroes, and in
forbidding free Negroes from crossing state lines. Free states also
had laws forbidding free Negroes from entering. But above all, the
South had decided, in the wake of the Wilmot Proviso controversy,
that new slave states must, from time to time, be added to the
Union, to balance the growing power of the free states within the
federal structure. However impossible such balance might be in the
House, it must at least be preserved in the Senate. Ironically
enough—from the viewpoint of Kendall and Carey—Southern
orators constantly appealed to Equality. They said the South must
have Equality with the North, the slave states must have Equality

with the free states. To have less than Equality meant degradation and—yes—slavery. And to that they would never submit. But if there were to be new slave states, slaveholders must enter the territories during their formative period and control the drafting of the state constitutions with which the new states would apply to Congress for admission. But as time and experience showed, the legal right of entrance was not enough. Slavery was a fragile institution. Stray slaves were not like stray cattle. They had heads as well as legs, and it required an enormously complicated system of slave patrols, of police regulations integrated into a pro-slavery society, to keep slaves working in their places and to make slavery economically viable. And so the doctrine developed that came to quintessential expression in Taney's opinion in the case of *Dred Scott*.[26] That opinion held not only that every slaveholder had a constitutional right to migrate with his slaves to any federal territory that was open to settlement, but also that the sole power that Congress had over the subject of slavery was the power *coupled with the duty* to protect the slaveowner in the exercise of his rights. It was this that brought about the sectional crisis in its final form. Whether Kendall was simply ignorant of the history of the period, or only pretended to be so, we do not know. But in no just sense was it "Lincoln's terms" which determined the crisis of 1860. Secession actually began when the Southern radicals walked out of the Democratic Convention. And they walked out when *Stephen A. Douglas*, and *his* supporters *in the Democratic* Party, refused to countenance the demand for a federal slave code. The demand for a federal slave code had exactly the same status in the North that a demand for emancipation would have had in the South. No politician could survive one moment who gave it a moment's countenance.

The Civil War came then not, as Kendall seems to suppose, merely because the Republican Party, a free-soil party, had elected Abraham Lincoln president. Lincoln wished to have federal law forbid slavery in federal territories. In this he differed from Douglas, who wished to permit the settlers to decide for themselves whether they would have freedom or slavery. But by 1860 the South had rejected Douglas as completely as they had rejected Lincoln. In some ways he was more hated, as they regarded him a traitor to their cause. Nothing less than "affirmative action" guaranteeing slavery in the territories would have kept the South in the Charleston Convention; nothing less would have averted secession after Lincoln's election.

We come finally to Kendall's assertion that the South was "entitled to secede if the issue was to be drawn on Lincoln's terms."[27] We have just seen that it was not Lincoln who drew the terms of the issue. Even if one wishes—however extravagantly—to place all responsibility in the North, it was the Northern Democracy no less than the Republicans who shared it. And the overwhelming majority of Democrats, led by Douglas, opposed secession as much as Lincoln. We might argue the case against secession in the familiar terms of national supremacy versus state rights. We might easily demonstrate why the "national" interest of the North made inconceivable the surrender of the navigation of the Mississippi to a foreign power and why the land-locked midwest in particular—the section from which Lincoln came—could never contemplate the alliance of an independent and hostile Confederacy with British Canada. But we think the issue is simpler even than these obvious political considerations.

In his inaugural address, Lincoln pointed out that the two sections could not, physically speaking, separate. Political separation, far from solving any problems, would make them all more acute. The fugitive slave law, now imperfectly enforced, would then not be enforced at all. The foreign slave trade, now imperfectly suppressed, might be openly revived. But above all, what would be done about the territories? The territories belonged to the United States. Would the South surrender its share in them in quitting the Union? If so, why secede? Would the North, recognizing the Confederacy, agree to divide the territories? If so, why not cease to resist the extension of slavery—and in particular the extension below 36 degrees 30 minutes, the Missouri Compromise line, as in the Crittenden Compromise—and keep the seceding states in the Union? In short, it would have been senseless for Lincoln to have resolutely opposed the extension of slavery and then to have agreed to secession—as Kendall proposes. For secession, had it succeeded, would have emancipated the South from nearly all restrictions upon

31

the extension and perpetuation of slavery. Unless the South was willing to fight the North for the territories, it made no sense for them to secede. Unless the North was willing to fight against secession, it made no sense to stand firm against the extension of slavery into the territories. To agree to secession, after not agreeing to slavery extension, would only have made the war much harder to win, without making it any less necessary. Surely Kendall must have seen that. There is not doubt that Lincoln did!

9.

According to Kendall and Carey, the supreme "symbol" of the American political traditions is the virtuous people, or the representatives of the virtuous people, deliberating under God. We have no quarrel with this formulation, as far as it goes. We prefer, on the whole, to speak of the principles of the tradition, rather than its symbols. We propose to prove by the American political tradition, that a people become a people only by virtue of the principle of Equality. Here we would point out that it was this same American people, deliberating according to the laws laid down in the Constitution, laws to which all equally had consented, that elected Abraham Lincoln President of the United States. No violence was used in this election, unless it was in the South, where there were no electors for Lincoln. No one has ever been entitled to take office according to the canons of consensus laid down by Kendall and Carey, if it was not Lincoln. Did he not appeal to the "basic symbols" precisely in their sense when he spoke these fateful lines on March 4, 1861?

> Why should there not be a patient confidence in the ultimate justice of the people? Is there any better, or equal hope, in the world?. . . . If the Almighty Ruler of nations, with his eternal truth and justice, be on your side of the North, or on yours of the South, that truth, and that justice, will surely prevail, by the judgment of this great tribunal, the American people.[28]

Was not the decision of the seceding states, to break up the government, rather than submit to Lincoln's election, a defiance of the virtuous people, deliberating according to the rules of the Constitution, and under God? Was not that election a decision by a constitutional majority, in which all rights of constitutional minorities had been carefully preserved? Had not Lincoln sworn an oath, before God and the people, to "take Care that the Laws be faithfully

executed" and to "preserve, protect, and defend the Constitution"?
How can Kendall—how can anyone—call Lincoln's fidelity to that
oath, incorporating as it does all that is sacred to the American
political tradition, "imposing one's own view concerning natural
right upon others"?[29]

Kendall thought that Jaffa would "launch [his readers] and with
them the nation upon a political future the very thought of which is
hair-raising. . . ."[30] This future would be made up

> of an endless series of Abraham Lincolns, each persuaded that he is superior
> in wisdom and virtue to the Fathers, each prepared to insist that those who
> oppose this or that new application of the equality standard are denying the
> possibility of self-government, each ultimately willing to plunge America
> into Civil War rather than concede his point. . . .[31]

My readers will by now perceive that this is good Confederate
caricature suitable for declamation—after playing "Dixie"—at a
meeting decorated by the stars and bars. The warning strikes me as
somewhat extravagant, given the number of my readers and the
magnitude of the intellectual demands that Kendall says my book
puts upon them. Kendall's premise seems to be that Lincoln—or
anyone—who opposed American slavery thereby favored each and
every "application of the equality standard." But this standard, we
are also told, leads to "the cooperative commonwealth of men who
will be so equal that no one will be able to tell them apart."[32] In
short, it will lead to the modern totalitarian slave state. Kendall's
case against Lincoln then comes down to this: Lincoln's opposition
to slavery leads to slavery.

Now, even if this were not self-contradictory, we would have
the right to ask, why is the slavery to which Lincoln leads us worse
than that which he helped to end? But of course, we are faced here
with a play on words, or a confusion of two meanings of Equality.
Lincoln never sought, or believed in, an equality of *condition*. What
he did believe in was an quality of *rights*. Over and over again, he
denied that he thought that men were equal in wisdom, virtue, or
ability, or that they should all have the same rewards. Lincoln said
in 1858:

> Certainly the negro is not our equal in color—perhaps not in many other
> respects; still, in the right to put into his mouth the bread that his own hands
> have earned, he is the equal of every other man. . . . In pointing out that

> more has been given [to] you, you cannot be justified in taking away the little which has been given [to] him. All I ask for the negro is that if you do not like him, let him alone. If God gave him little . . . that little let him enjoy.[33]

Surely no simpler nor more eloquent appeal ever was made to the principles of natural justice. Equality here meant nothing more than the equal right of all men to be treated justly. In his message to Congress of July 4, 1861, Lincoln defined the cause of the Union. It was, he said, to maintain in the world

> that form, and substance of government, whose leading object is, to elevate the condition of men—to lift artificial weights from all shoulders—to clear the paths of laudable pursuit for all—to afford all, an unfettered start, and a fair chance, in the race of life.[34]

Kendall and Carey refer repeatedly to Lincoln having "curious" notions of what Equality meant which, they say, "even his worshippers cannot deny."[35] But, curiously enough, they give no explanation whatever of this assertion. One of the speeches which they list as supporting this contention is the one from which we have just quoted. Is giving everyone an *unfettered* start and a fair chance what is "curious"? Is not this the idea behind the Statue of Liberty? Is it curious that we should be proud to call ourselves the land, not of the slave, but of the free? Have we not been the Promised Land for countless millions who have fled from persecution and oppression in the Egypt of the Old World? Was it not always an anomaly for the Promised Land itself to have slavery? And is not Abraham Lincoln himself the very most "basic symbol" within the American political tradition of personal self-reliance, of bootstrap individualism? In this connection we cannot refrain from telling one of our favorite Lincoln stories. A visitor came into his office in the White House one day to find him blacking his boots. "Why, Mr. President," the astonished man exclaimed, "do you black your own boots?" "Whose boots do you think I black?" growled Lincoln.

10.

We observed that Kendall and Carey never, to our knowledge, mention slavery in *Basic Symbols*. But the following passage seems to elevate Inequality to the status we had thought belonged to its opposite.

34

II. Equality as a Conservative Principle

> Is the American political tradition [they ask] the tradition of the textbooks, which indeed situates the "all men are created equal" clause at the center of our political experience, *or is it the tradition of American life as it is actually lived and thus a tradition of inequality?*[36]

Here Kendall and Carey confuse the "is" with the "ought" of a political tradition. "Life as it is actually lived" should refer not only to what people *do*, but also to the ethical norms or imperatives by which they understand the meaning of what they do. Kendall and Carey refer repeatedly to the American people as being a Christian people. Would they identify Christians solely by their observance of the golden rule, *i.e.*, only by their lives as they are "actually [*i.e.*, selfishly] lived"?

Kendall, we noted, thinks that Lincoln (and Jaffa) points us toward a state of society in which men are "so equal that no one will be able to tell them apart." Yet were not all slaves equally denied the privileges of freedom, without regard to age, sex, virtue, or intelligence? Did they not all receive the same "wages," regardless of how much or how little they worked? Kendall and Carey speak—inaccurately—of the Declaration of Independence as referring to a Christian people. Christianity is a revealed religion. But in its references to "self-evident" truths and to "Nature" and "Nature's God," the Declaration certainly has reference to natural, not to revealed theology. Still, the moral commands of the Decalogue are held by many Christians to be knowable by unassisted human reason as well as by Biblical revelation. And American slavery was as much an institutionalized denial of the moral claims of the Ten Commandments as Hitler's concentration camps or the Gulag Archipelago. Since slaves were legally chattels, they could make no legal contracts, including marriage. How could children honor their fathers and mothers, when the fathers and mothers were not lawfully married, when they had no lawful power over their children, and when they could not acquire any of the property which is at the foundation of family life? How could the prohibition against adultery be regarded, when there was no lawful distinction between fornication and adultery? How could chastity be a virtue for those who had no lawful power over their own bodies? How could prohibitions against covetousness and theft be addressed to those who could possess no

35

property and all the fruits of whose labor were taken from them? How could slaves regard the injunction against bearing false witness, when their testimony could never be given in court against white men? And did not the example of Moses, who had killed a slave master, justify any one in striking down another who obstructed his path to freedom?

American slavery treated all men of a certain class as having their worth determined by their membership in that class. This is equally the root of contemporary totalitarianism. To be elevated, or regarded as worthy, because one is white, proletarian, or Aryan, or to be degraded and scorned as a Negro, a capitalist, or a Jew, does not involve any ultimate distinction of principle. Kendall's denunciation of the "cooperative commonwealth" of those whose identities are lost in "equality" is utterly stultified by his refusal to condemn American slavery and by his condemnation of Lincoln for condemning it.

The "real" American political tradition, say Kendall and Carey, is not one of Equality. Except in the form of a rhetorical question, they do not positively assert that it is one of Inequality. Putting together their various formulations, *the* "basic symbols" of our tradition are—or is—the representative assembly (or assemblies) of the virtuous people deliberating under God. (There is the same difficulty with singular and plural here, as in the case of The United States.) We have no quarrel with the emphasis they place upon deliberation, or upon the need for morality and religion among the institutions of a *free* people. We think there is a fundamental misunderstanding implied in their case for legislative supremacy among the three branches of government. We think they confuse the supremacy of legislation, conceived as an act of the sovereign people in its constitution-making role, and legislation as an exercise of the ordinary powers of government provided by the Constitution. But this difference arises from the far more fundamental difference we have, concerning what it is that makes discrete individuals into a sovereign people, and hence what it is that authorizes any people to institute government, "laying its foundation on such principles and organizing its powers in such form, as to them shall seem most likely to effect their Safety and Happiness." Kendall and Carey assume the existence of the people, and never ask what it is, from the viewpoint of the Founding Fathers, that entitled the American people to consider themselves as sovereign. But the answer to that question, as we propose to demonstrate, is Equality.

The Declaration of Independence, of course, affirms it to be a self-evident truth, "that all men are created equal." Within short intervals during the Revolution, the people of the several states adopted new constitutions. Most of these contained preambles, bills or declarations of rights, which gave the "foundation of principles" upon which they were to erect the "forms" of government they thought most likely to effect their safety and happiness. For example, Virginia stated "That all men are by nature equally free and independent"; Pennsylvania, "That all men are born equally free and independent"; Vermont, "That all men are born equally free and independent"; Massachusetts, that "All men are born free and equal"; New Hampshire, that "All men are born equally free and independent"; Delaware, "That all government of right originates from the people [and] is founded in compact only. . . ."[37] Maryland also said "that all government of right originates from the people, [and] is founded in compact only. . . ."[38]

Now we contend that all these statements of principle, where they are not verbally identical, all mean one and the same thing. It will be observed that Virginia, Pennsylvania, Vermont, and New Hampshire say "equally free and independent." Massachusetts says "free and equal." Clearly, "equal" and "independent" mean the same thing. Also, "born" and "by nature" mean the same thing. Delaware and Maryland vary this language slightly by saying that rightful government is "founded in compact only." This expression, we shall see, means simply that government is the result of an agreement by men who were originally, or by nature, or born, equally free and independent. Jefferson's "created equal" is simply the most succinct formulation of this commonly understood doctrine.

Willmoore Kendall devoted the last years of his life to an extraordinary effort to read John Locke out of the American political tradition. That there was a compact theory much older than the American, he knew. That Socrates had appealed to one, he knew from the *Crito* of Plato. But he didn't trust the Old Pagan, as "The

People versus Socrates Revisited" showed. With a great swoop, he lighted finally upon the Mayflower Compact. Here he found at last, if not a compact theory, at least a compact. No matter, if the Pilgrims didn't have a theory, Kendall would supply it to them! The important thing was that there was not a word in the Mayflower Compact about Equality, and there was something—not much, but something—about "advancing the Christian faith." So Kendall labelled his second chapter in *Basic Symbols* "In the Beginning: The Mayflower Compact," and tried to prove that the Founding Fathers—who were now, in fact, the Founding Great-great-great-great-Grandsons—had always meant substantially what the men of the Mayflower Compact had meant. That is to say, they had meant what they would or could or should have meant if they too had been born before John Locke. But all this effort was in vain. While we would never contend that there are *no* non-Lockean elements in the Founding, or that the Founding Fathers always interpreted the Lockean elements in a Lockean manner, Locke is nonetheless there. The primary appeals to principles in the Revolution are Lockean. The principle of limited, constitutional government, by which the Fathers rejected despotism and by which they constructed their own governments, were fundamentally Lockean. Without understanding this, no other aspects of the Revolution, or of the American political tradition, are intelligible.

The spirit of Locke's political teaching is conveyed well by the opening sentence of his *First Treatise:* "Slavery is so vile and miserable an estate of man, and so directly opposite to the generous temper and courage of our nation, that it is hardly to be conceived that an Englishman, much less a gentleman, should plead for it."[39] The major part of the treatise is devoted to a refutation of Sir Robert Filmer's *Patriarcha* (1680), a work which attempts to found absolute monarchy upon a title derived from Adam. Locke demonstrates the absurdity of such a title, not to mention the difficulty of finding its rightful possessor! But consider the language of the Continental Congress, in the Declaration of the Causes and Necessity of Taking Up Arms, July 6, 1775:

> If it was possible for men, who exercise their reason to believe, that the divine Author of our existence intended a part of the human race to hold an

38

absolute property in, and an unbounded power over others . . . the inhabitants of these colonies might at least require from the parliament of Great
Britain some evidence, that this dreadful authority over them, has been
granted to that body.[40]

Did ever a great revolution in human affairs ever begin with such
sarcasm? Can one not hear the very accents of Locke's *First Treatise*
as he rakes old Filmer over the coals? One thinks, for example, of
Sir Robert's derivation of kingly power from paternal power, citing
the Biblical injunction to honor one's father. To this Locke retorted
with evident glee that the Bible speaks of honoring one's father *and
mother* and asks why Sir Robert does not find queenly as well as
kingly authority in such injunctions. But the Continental Congress,
in rejecting the proposition that any part of the *human race* (not
merely Englishmen *vis-à-vis* Englishmen) might hold a right of
property in any other part, clearly condemned in principle *all*
slavery. And this they might do, only if, in their right to non-despotic rule, *all men are equal.*

   In his attack on Filmer, Locke characterizes his "system" in this
"little compass." "[I]t is," says Locke, "no more but this":

> *That all government is absolute monarchy.*[41]

"And the ground he builds on is this":

> *That no man is born free.*[42]

Robert A. Goldwin observes that "Locke's own political teaching
may be stated in opposite terms but with similar brevity. . . ."[43]
Goldwin's first Lockean proposition is this:

> *All government is limited in its powers and
> exists only by the consent of the governed.*[44]

And, says Goldwin, the ground Locke builds on is this:

> *All men are born free.*[45]

The argument for absolute monarchy—or despotism, for they are
the same—is grounded in Locke in the proposition that no man is
born free. The argument for limited government (or constitutional
government, for they are the same) is grounded in Locke in the
proposition that all men are born free. But we shall see that in

Locke—and *in the nature of things*—the proposition that all men are born free is itself an inference from the proposition that all men are born equal. The equality of all men by nature and the freedom of all men by nature differ as the concavity of a curved line differs from its convexity. The two are distinguishable, but inseparable.

Let us now turn to the famous passage in *The Second Treatise*, in which Locke considers "what state all men are naturally in."[46] It is, he says,

> a state of perfect freedom to order their actions and dispose of their possessions and persons as they think fit, within the bounds of the law of nature, without asking leave or depending upon the will of any other man.[47]

But it is also, he continues,

> [a] state . . . of equality, wherein all the power and jurisdiction is reciprocal, no one having more than another; there being nothing more evident than [meaning thereby that it is self-evident] that creatures of the same species and rank . . . should also be equal one amongst another without subordination and subjection. . . .[48]

We would re-phrase Locke's argument as follows: there is no difference between man and man as there is between man and, for example, dog, such that one is recognizable as the other's natural superior. And if men are not *naturally* subordinate, one to another—as all the brute creation are *naturally* subordinate to man—then they are *naturally* not in a state of government, or civil society. They are, instead, *naturally* free and independent, or *born* free and independent. But they are born free and independent, *because* they are born—or created—equal.

There can be no question—and Kendall and Carey do not question—that the just powers of government in the American political tradition are derived from the consent of the governed. Kendall and Carey treat consent however as if it were an ultimate and not a derived principle. But that is not the way Locke or the Founders treated it. They derived it from man's natural freedom and equality. It is the recognition of Equality which not only gives rise to consent, but also which provides consent with a positive content of meaning. Kendall and Carey, by allowing consent to stand alone, as if it were an ultimate principle, have no basis for saying what it is to which men might reasonably consent. In 1854, Lincoln quoted his notable antagonist thus:

> Judge Douglas frequently, with bitter irony and sarcasm, paraphrases our argument by saying: "The white people of Nebraska are good enough to govern themselves, *but they are not good enough to govern a few miserable negroes!!*"
>
> Well, I doubt not that the people of Nebraska are, and will continue to be as good as the average of people elsewhere. I do not say the contrary. What I do say is, that no man is good enough to govern another man, *without that other's consent.*[49]

Kendall and Carey, like Douglas, do not see that the people's right to give their consent is itself derived from the equality of *all* men and therefore limits and directs what it is to which they may rightfully consent. Their view leads to the conclusion that whatever any particular people may be persuaded by demagogues to agree or consent to, becomes "right." Calling the people "virtuous" and saying that they deliberate "under God" may become a mere cloak for vice and hypocrisy, as our examination of the ethics of slavery showed.

That men are by nature free and equal is the ground simultaneously of political obligation—of consent as the immediate source of the just powers of government—and of a doctrine of limited government and of an ethical code. Because man is by nature a rational being, he may not rule other rational beings as if they were mere brutes. Because man is not all-wise or all-powerful, because his reason is swayed by his passions, he may not be a judge in his own cause, and he may *not* therefore rule other men despotically. Men do not need the consent of brute creation to rule over it. Nor does God need the consent of men rightfully to exercise his Providential rule over them. Man is the in-between being, between beast and God, "a little lower than the angels." Consent is that ground of obligation which corresponds with this "in-betweenness." It is the contemplation of this universe, articulated as it is into the intelligible hierarchy of beast, man, and God, which not only brings consent as a principle into view, but also enlightens it, and brings it thereby into harmony with "the Laws of Nature and of Nature's God." To repeat, the proposition that all men are created equal implies an understanding of man, in the light of the universe, in the light of the distinction between the human and the subhuman on the one hand, and of the human and the superhuman on the other. As we have already observed, it does *not*, for this reason, ignore the very important differences between man and man. On the contrary, it is for the sake of those differences that it denies any man the right to rule others, *as if* those others were beasts. And there are no standing rules, and impartial judges, to govern the differences between slaves and their owners and masters. For the rule of a master to be a matter of right, the master would have to differ from the servant, as God is supposed to differ from man. Whatever one's beliefs as to the *existence* of Divinity, it is evident—or self-evident—that no man possesses that power or wisdom which we suppose that God—if He exists—possesses. While not supposing for a moment that the Founders did not believe in the actual existence of God, their assumptions about Equality—which include assumptions about the subhuman and the superhuman—are independent of the validity of any particular religious beliefs. In the decisive respect, their assumptions are not assumptions at all, but observations of a world in which the difference between men and beasts provides a clear and distinct idea of what the Divine nature, in its politically relevant aspects, must be.

Kendall and Carey suppose that the constitutional morality of *The Federalist* has nothing whatever to do with Equality. That they are wrong becomes clear the moment one understands that the proposition that all men are created equal is not about man alone, but about man, God, and Nature; and that Nature implies the difference between the human and the sub-human, as well as that between the human and the super-human. Consider the famous passage of Madison's in the fifty-first *Federalist*:

> If men were angels, no government would be necessary. If angels were to govern men, neither external nor internal controls on government would be necessary. In framing a government which is to be administered by men over men, the great difficulty lies in this: you must first enable the government to control the governed; and in the next place oblige it to control itself.[50]

Here the very nature of the problem that constitutionalism is meant to solve is determined by the meaning of Equality.

But does not constitutionalism imply an ethics as well as a

politics? Do we not recognize that the equality of all men by nature, leading as it does to civil society, is the justification for the *inequalities* of civil society? Do we not thereby see that officials are but men and must live under the laws that they make and administer? (Abraham Lincoln: "The master not only governs the slave without his consent; but he governs him by a set of rules altogether different from those which he prescribes for himself"[51]) Do we not recognize that *our* consent makes *their* acts lawful, and that in obeying them, we are not deferring to our superiors in nature, but only to the principle of authority that is in ourselves? Is it not this that makes obedience not demeaning (not slavish), but dignified, and sometimes even noble? But still further, does not Equality, which makes *our* consent necessary to the laws *we* obey, oblige us to recognize the *same* rights in *other* men? Does it not also tell us that we may not consider other men mere means to our ends—as we may consider the brute creation—or as we may be considered by a Divine Providence whose power and wisdom so far transcends our own? (Are we not taught by Revelation that God does *not* consider us as mere means, but that this is not necessary to his being, but represents the miracle of His grace?) Do not all the totalitarian slave states of our time rest upon theoretical propositions in which race or class differences delude some men to consider themselves superhuman? And does not this delusion lie at the root of their bestiality? Is it not this that makes them think that, for the sake of the classless society, or the thousand year Reich, everything is permitted to them? Surely Abraham Lincoln was right when he said that the doctrine of human equality was "the father of all moral principle [amongst] us."[52]

11.

There is a tendency among Conservatives to identify Equality with some species of socialism or—in Kendall's words—with "the cooperative commonwealth of men who will be so equal that no one will be able to tell them apart." But the doctrine of Equality, in particular in its Lockean sense, is essential to the defense of the institution of private property in the modern world. For the doctrine of Equality holds that what men are by nature, that is, prior to civil society, determines what purposes civil society may rightfully serve.

It is this that determines what rights are inalienable, and what rights may—or must—reasonably be surrendered to society. It was axiomatic for the Founders that the rights of conscience were never surrendered to civil society, and that therefore civil society might never rightfully enact laws in matters that were wholly and exclusively matters of conscience. It took more than a generation after the Revolution to uproot all the colonial laws which, directly or indirectly, "established" religion, by giving one or another religious belief the assistance of law. Moreover, the determined way in which men like Jefferson and Madison acted to get rid, not only of religious establishment in all its forms, but also of such vestiges of feudal law as primogeniture and entail, proves how little regard they had for that colonial past Kendall tried to make the ground of the American political tradition.

Primogeniture and entail were anachronisms on the American scene. They were essentially limitations upon the right of a man to control his own property and to dispose of it at his pleasure. They were props of aristocracy, inimical to the spirit both of democracy and of capitalism. They were, so to speak, elements of a "Tory socialism." But Locke had taught that men were by nature property-acquiring animals. He had taught that both life and liberty became valuable and were themselves natural rights, above all because they culminated in the possession and enjoyment of property. No one in America who heard the Declaration of Independence read out for the first time had any doubt that pursuing happiness meant primarily, as Virginia had already put it, "acquiring and possessing property." It was because the Parliament of Great Britain had appeared to assert a right to tax the colonists without their consent by making laws and statutes "in all cases whatsoever," that they had revolted. But men like George Washington—as vigorous a land speculator as ever lived—were driven into rebellion in part by their inability to get the government at Westminster to grant patents and titles to the land they had surveyed in such places as the Ohio valley. Government, in their view, existed to facilitate the acquisition and enjoyment of private property. Such property might be taxed—with their consent—so that the government might be able to protect that same property. But it might not tax them to

44

render nugatory, in any manner or sense, their efforts *in* acquiring and possessing property. The principle of Equality, far from enfranchising any leveling action of government, is the ground for the recognition of those human differences which arise *naturally*, but in *civil society*, when human industry and acquisitiveness are emancipated. We saw that Madison reflected the doctrine of Equality, when he attributed the need for constitutional government, and constitutional morality, to the difference between men and angels. But he reflected it no less when, in the tenth *Federalist*, he put as the *"first* object of government," the protection "of different and *unequal* faculties of acquiring property. . . ."[53] In his *Second Treatise*, Locke had put the origin of property in human labor. It was the natural right—the equal right—which each man had to his own body, and therefore to the labor of that body, that was the ultimate foundation of the right to private property in civil society. How can Kendall and Carey not have seen, as Lincoln saw, that the denial of Equality was the denial of the principle upon which private property, as well as every other personal freedom, rested? Nothing illustrates better Lincoln's egalitarianism, and his attitude toward property, than the following message, which he sent to a meeting of the Workingmen's Association in New York, during the Civil War:

> Let not him who is houseless [wrote Lincoln] pull down the house of another; but let him labor diligently and build one for himself, thus by example assuring that his own [house] shall be safe from violence when built.[54]

Surely here is the wisdom of Solomon and of a just and generous Conservatism.

12.

We turn finally to two myths propagated by Kendall and Carey which, it seems to us, have been stumbling blocks for American Conservatives—particularly for those who have forgotten their American history. According to *Basic Symbols* it was Lincoln who somehow invented a *"constitutional status"* for the Declaration and, by his enumeration of "four score and seven years" in the Gettysburg Address, spuriously caused the occasion for Independence to become that of our birth *"as a nation."* What was established on July 4, 1776, they say, was not a nation, but only "a baker's dozen of new sovereignties."[55] In short, what the thirteen colonies did that day was not merely to declare themselves independent of Great Britain, but to declare themselves independent of each other. Here is Lincoln, taking up that claim, in his message to Congress, July 4, 1861.

> Therein [that is, by the Declaration of Independence] the "United Colonies" were declared to be "Free and Independent States"; but, even then, the object plainly was not to declare their independence of *one another*, or of the *Union*; but directly the contrary, as their mutual pledge, and their mutual action, before, at the time, and afterwards, abundantly show.[56]

How can Kendall and Carey revive this old Confederate propaganda without even alluding to the "abundant" evidence with which Lincoln had refuted it?

However indeterminate the character of American federalism may have been at that early date, there can be no question but that the thirteen former colonies, now states, remained united, and always, before the rest of the world, assumed the character of a single person. Passing over the pledge of unity in the Declaration itself, and the further pledge in the Articles of Confederation that the Union shall be perpetual, we would direct attention to Article VI of the Constitution. It declares that "All Debts contracted and Engagements entered into, before the Adoption of this Constitution, shall be as valid against the United States under this Constitution, as under the Confederation." Thus the United States "before the Adoption of this Constitution," the United States "under the Confederation," and the United States "under this Constitution," are all *the same United States.* According to Article VI, the one from which the many were formed—according to *et pluribus unum*, the motto of the United States—did not result from the Constitution. But if the Constitution did not cause the Union, then the Union (that is the Union of the People of the United States) must have caused the Constitution. But if the Union as a sovereign entity had an origin before 1787, when else can it have been except on July 4, 1776? If the Declaration gave birth to the Union which gave birth to the Constitution, it must itself have *constitutional status.*[57] And so it always has had in the statutes of the United States. Lincoln was of course perfectly correct in what he said at Gettysburg, and elsewhere, upon this topic.

II. Equality as a Conservative Principle

But is it proper to refer to the Union which came into being in 1776 as a *nation*? Certainly neither Union nor nation were fully formed—any more than any other infant—at birth. But Thomas Jefferson, writing to James Madison, on August 30, 1823, referred without hesitation to a meeting that had taken place in the previous month, as "an anniversary assemblage of the nation on its birthday."[58] I would venture to doubt whether anyone can find any expression by any American statesman during the first fifty years following independence that contradicts the opinion that July 4, 1776, was the birthday *of the nation*. These were the formative years of Lincoln's life. He grew up, strange to say, believing what Jefferson said about our being a nation, just as he grew up believing Jefferson when he wrote "that all men are created equal."

We come now to Kendall and Carey's contention that Equality, which had admittedly (and unfortunately) loomed so large in the Declaration, had somehow disappeared when the Constitution, and the federal bill of rights, came to be written. Our readers will readily perceive that this alleged omission *is* an omission, only if the Declaration itself lacked *constitutional status*. But we have just proved that it *does* have that *status*. The Declaration authorized each of the thirteen states separately, and all of them collectively, to "institute new Government" such as to them "shall seem most likely to effect their Safety and Happiness." The statement of principles in the Declaration of Independence properly accompanied a revolutionary change in political allegiance. It also properly accompanied a dissolution of one social compact and the formation of another (or others). There was a good deal of contemporaneous discussion as to whether the dissolving of the political allegiance of the colonists to the British crown also constituted a dissolution of the social compact among themselves. According to James Madison, "The question was brought before Congress at its first session by Doctor Ramsay, who contested the election of William Smith; who, though born in South Carolina, had been absent at the date of independence. The decision was, that his birth in the Colony made him a member of society in its new as well as its original state."[59] We can easily imagine some Tories, who were driven out of the country, contesting this decision! In any event, there was no such revolutionary change as occurred in 1776, in the interval between 1776

47

and 1787. The absence of a new declaration of principles in 1787, far from indicating that the Framers had forgotten the old one, is a sign that they remembered it perfectly. Had they changed their minds about those principles in any way, a new one might have been indicated. But they had not changed their minds, and the country that ratified the Constitution understood perfectly that the principles of 1776, as expressed not only in the national Declaration of Independence, but also in all the state declarations accompanying the state constitutions, governed the new Constitution as well.

The principles of the Declaration are not, however, merely presupposed in the Constitution. They are present in the very first words of the Constitution as those words were understood by those who drafted and adopted it. "We the People of the United States," implies the existence of a *compact* in precisely the sense in which Delaware and Maryland used that term in their declarations of rights. In the debates on nullification, in the early 1830s, speakers on all sides of that difficult question, prefaced their remarks by saying that compact was the basis of all free government. In one of his last writings, an essay on "Sovereignty," Madison affirmed as a matter of course "that all power in just and free governments is derived from compact."[69] By compact, he said, he meant "the theory which contemplates a certain number of individuals as meeting and agreeing to form one political society, in order that the rights, the safety, and the interest of each my be under the safeguard of the whole."[61] "The first supposition" of such an agreement, said Madison, "is that each individual being previously independent of the others, the compact which is to make them one society must result from the free consent of *every* individual."[62] If then the people of the United States, who ordained the Constitution of the United States, are a free people, they must have been formed into civil society by the free consent of *every* individual. But that would not be possible unless every individual, then and since, forming part of the people of the United States, like all mankind, in the original and originating sense, had been by the laws of nature and of nature's God, "created equal."

III. How to Think
About the American Revolution:
A Bicentennial Cerebration

IN WHAT MAY BE THE MOST AMBITIOUS AND PRESTIGIOUS EFFORT of its kind, the American Enterprise Institute has sponsored a Distinguished Lecture Series on the Bicentennial of the United States. A number of notable Americans were asked to deliver their thoughts upon the American Revolution. Each lecture was treated as a ceremonial occasion of great dignity. Each was given at some historic, or quasi–historic site. Each was published separately as a pamphlet, although they were later gathered into a single volume.[1] The lectures were recorded on film, and broadcast on educational television throughout the nation. Excerpts have been syndicated in the newspapers. The printing of the pamphlets is exquisite, and the rough cut rag paper that of the finest limited editions. Inside the front cover each speaker is shown at his lectern, in a photograph of chromatic blue upon a cream–white background, with the base lettering in red. Inside the back cover is a full photograph, also in blue, of the building in which the lecture was delivered. Medallions, seals, and mottoes adorn the whole. Sure American Enterprise's genius for packaging its products has never been displayed to better advantage.

> A word fitly spoken, is like apples of gold
> in pictures of silver. *Proverbs*, 25: 11[2]

Our concern however will be, not with the silver ornament, but with the golden apples. Are the words fitly spoken? Are the apples indeed of gold?

Leo Strauss used to delight in pointing out that the most conservative or even reactionary organization in the United States was called the Daughters of the American Revolution. The D.A.R. has not been much in the news of late, and I do not know whether it still deserves the distinction Strauss accorded it. The American Enterprise Institute, although certainly not reactionary, and having nothing, so to speak, in common with the D.A.R., is nevertheless known as a conservative institution. It is not surprising therefore that the speakers selected to sound the inaugural themes of the Distinguished Lecture Series—Professors Irving Kristol and Martin Diamond—should offer interpretations of the Revolution eminently conservative. Professor Kristol's Distinguished Lecture is entitled "The American Revolution as a Successful Revolution." Professor Diamond's is entitled "The Revolution of Sober Expectations." Success and Sobriety. Here above all are the qualities that conservatives recognize as their own. We can distill the message of these two Distinguished Lectures by saying that the American Revolution was successful because it was sober. But sobriety and revolution do not, in the common understanding, sit well together. Professor Kristol's task therefore was to sever the link connecting the idea of revolution with that of an unsober and impractical enthusiasm. The theme of his Distinguished Lecture is that what made our revolution a success is that it was as unlike as possible any of the other great revolutions of the last two centuries. What made it so unlike, is that it aimed at being as little revolutionary as possible. It is not overstating Professor Kristol's case to say that in his view the American Revolution was intended to preserve the *status quo*. ". . . [A] successful revolution," he writes, "is best accomplished by a people who do not really want it at all, but find themselves reluctantly making it. The American Revolution was exactly such a reluctant revolution."[3]

Professor Kristol further vindicates the unrevolutionary character of the American Revolution by drawing a distinction borrowed from Hannah Arendt's *On Revolution*. In this work, there is said to be a fundamental difference between "revolution" and "rebellion." The French and Russian revolutions, we are told, "should more properly be called 'rebellions,' whereas only the American Revolution is worthy of the name."[4] This, we cannot forbear remarking, should have made any D.A.R. members present completely happy. A rebellion, it seems, is not a political event at all, but rather something "meta-political." It emerges "out of a radical dissatisfac-

tion with the human condition." Its spirit is "a spirit of despera-
tion—a desperate rejection of whatever exists, a desperate aspira-
tion towards some kind of utopia."[5] But the intentions of a rebellion
are "impossible" and hence "unrealizable." Because of this disap-
pointment is inevitable. But the enthusiasts of rebellion are true
believers. *Credunt quia absurdum est.* They cannot admit that the
defect lies in the contradictions embodied in their faith. And so they
are driven to find heresy and treason within the ranks of the alleged
votaries of that faith. The myth of "the revolution betrayed" arises
necessarily, and from it inquisitions and reigns of terror necessarily
follow. But a revolution properly so called is a "political phenomenon." It is a "practical exercise in political philosophy" which
revises and reorders "the political arrangements of a society." "It
requires attentive prudence, a careful calculation of means and
ends, a spirit of sobriety—the kind of spirit exemplified by that
calm, legalistic document, the Declaration of Independence."[6]

Professor Kristol ends his Distinguished Lecture by observing
that we today have in a sense become "victims of [the] success" of
the American Revolution. The system that resulted from it has
worked so well that we have ceased to inquire or to inform ourselves
why it has worked so well. But our ignorance is, so to speak, feeding
back into the system, which cannot go on working well with a citizen
body ill instructed in the principles of the system. Professor Kristol
thus leaves us with the hope that the Bicentennial will be more than
a mere celebration, but will lead to "a deeper and more widespread
understanding of just what it is we are celebrating."[7]

Surely nothing could be more pious or more just than such a
hope. But does Professor Kristol point us in the direction of the
understanding we need? Was the American Revolution indeed a
success? More precisely, was it a success for the reasons advanced
by Professor Kristol? These reasons are given most fully in the
following paragraph, which we quote at some length.

> To begin at the beginning: the American Revolution was successful in that
> those who led it were able, in later years, to look back in tranquillity at what
> they had wrought and to say that it was good. This was a revolution which,
> unlike all subsequent revolutions, did not devour its children: the men who
> made the revolution were the men who went on to create the new political

order, who then held the highest elected positions in this order, and who all died in bed. Not very romantic perhaps. Indeed, positively prosaic. But it is this very prosaic quality of the American Revolution that testifies to its success. It is the pathos and poignancy of unsuccessful revolutions which excite the poetic temperament; statesmanship which successfully accomplishes its business is a subject more fit for prose. Alone among the revolutions of modernity, the American Revolution did not give rise to the pathetic and poignant myth of "the revolution betrayed." It spawned no literature of disillusionment; it left behind no grand hopes frustrated, no grand expectations unsatisfied, no grand illusions shattered. Indeed, in one important respect the American Revolution was so successfull as to be almost self-defeating: it turned the attention of thinking men away from politics, which now seemed utterly unproblematic, so that political theory lost its vigor, and even the political thought of the Founding Fathers was not seriously studied. This intellectual sloth, engendered by success, rendered us incompetent to explain this successful revolution to the world, and even to ourselves. The American political tradition became an inarticulate tradition. . . .[8]

Surely this is one of the most striking passages in contemporary political literature. Professor Kristol writes so well in celebration of our inarticulate tradition that it seems almost churlish to ask exactly what he means. We are reminded of Aristotle's dictum, that poetry is truer than history. Still, it is primarily (but not exclusively) in its relationship to history that we propose to examine this—and related—paragraphs in Professor Kristol's Distinguished Lecture. In that light, we must say, it belongs in the library of American political mythology, alongside Parson Weems' patriotic tale of George Washington and the cherry tree.

Winston Churchill once remarked that chronology was the secret of successful political narration. Professor Kristol's chronology in his implied overview of American history, is a mystery if not a secret. He seems to say that, with the Founding Fathers serenely dead in bed, the American political scene became a humdrum routine. Politics, he says, "now seemed utterly unproblematic . . . and even the political thought of the Founding Fathers was not seriously studied." But when was—or is—the "now" to which Professor Kristol refers? 1798? 1800? 1832? 1850? 1933? 1975? Is American history a fairy tale, in which everyone lived happily ever after? Or did they live happily until one day they forgot they were happy, and so forgot as well the reason why?

If there is any amnesia in this story of America after the Revolution, it is Professor Kristol's omission of the Civil War from the perspective in which he views the American past. The American Revolution and the American Civil War were not merely discrete events. The one led directly to the other. They constitute the first and the last acts of a single drama. The fourscore and seven years between the Declaration of Independence and the Gettysburg Address comprehended the action of a tremendous world–historical tragedy. Indeed, in no other sequence of political events of which I know, did history and poetry so closely resemble each other. I would certainly agree with Professor Kristol that the outcome of the American Revolution was a success. It was a success, not for the reasons he gives, but because, as Lincoln had oberved in 1838, we lived under a political system conducing more to the ends of civil and religious liberty, than any which the history of former times had recorded. But such an achievement was not to be the prosaic comedy of Professor Kristol's imagination. The successful outcome resembled in the end far more that which we find at the end of *Macbeth* or *Hamlet*, when Scotland and Denmark are restored to political health by the pity and terror of a tragic consummation.

The American polity that was both generated by and that emerged from, what Allan Nevins has called the "Ordeal of Union," may indeed be the most successful the modern world has seen. But no one aware of that ordeal, or who has contemplated the dilemmas from which it sprung, can call American politics "unproblematic." If the generation of the Civil War was the offspring of that of the Revolution—the grandchildren if not the children—it must be acknowledged that the American Revolution, as much as any, devoured its progeny. Moreover, anyone familiar with antebellum politics, knows that the charge of the "revolution betrayed," in one form or another, dominated the rhetoric of political conflict. For example, we give an excerpt from the "Appeal of the Independent Democrats," January 19, 1854. This was the original appeal by the anti–slavery forces in Congress to the country, in opposition to the Kansas–Nebraska Bill, which had repealed the Missouri Compromise restriction upon slavery. It led to the formation of the "anti–Nebraska" coalition, out of which the Republican Party emerged.

> We arraign this bill as a gross violation of a sacred pledge; as a criminal betrayal of precious rights; as part and parcel of an atrocious plot to exclude from a vast unoccupied region immigrants from the Old World and free laborers from our own states, and to convert it into a dreary region of despotism. . . .[9]

Needless to say, equally harsh charges of bad faith were hurled back by the representatives of slaveholding states. During the four years from 1861 to 1865, more Americans died in war than in all other wars in American history combined, including both world wars of the twentieth century, up to an including the Korean War. And that was in a nation of thirty millions. The temperate view Professor Kristol takes of American political history is possible only if one keeps the Civil War discreetly out of sight.

One of the best works of American history of recent years is William W. Freehling's study of the nullification controversy in South Carolina, which reached a crisis in 1832. The title of that work is *Prelude to Civil War*.[10] Many other episodes of the fourscore and seven years could, with only differing degrees of propriety, claim a similar title. Among them would be the struggle over the Alien and Sedition Acts, comprehending the Kentucky and Virginia Resolutions, and the election of 1800, which Jefferson insisted was a greater revolution than that of 1776. That "revolution" saw Jefferson and Madison on one side and, until his death, Washington, together with Adams, Hamilton, and Marshall, on the other. But the struggle over Missouri, and the entire subsequent struggle over the territories, from the annexation of Texas and the Mexican War until the actual outbreak of the Civil War, were all "preludes."

Professor Kristol should have recalled Tocqueville's famous aphorism, that the Americans did not have to undergo a democratic revolution, that they were born equal without having to become so. It was for this reason that there could be no *immediate* parallel between the domestic disturbances of the American Revolution and the social convulsions of the great European revolutions. The Americans in 1776 withdrew their allegiance from an authority three thousand miles away, an authority represented for the most part by a mere handfull of royal officials. There were no great estates, secular and ecclesiastical, which formed the economic and social foundation of an oppressive and privileged order. There were no sharp class differences, no ancestral hatreds, that divided Patriots from Tories or Loyalists. Many of the Tories emigrated, but those who remained were soon indistinguishable from other Americans. In the French and Russian revolutions, animosities and passions nurtured and repressed over many centuries were unleased by the collapse of the *ancien régimes*. The comparative mildness of the struggle against the British arose from the fact that here there was no *ancien régime*, either to hate or to regret. The only proper point of comparison between the American and European revolutions with respect to their violence, their pathos, and their poignancy, is what happened in the overthrow of feudalism, on the one hand, and of slavery, on the other. Moreover, the full tale of removing the curse of American slavery extends far beyond even the Civil War, to the lynchings of the post–Reconstruction era, and to the racial strife of the twentieth century. In the Civil War itself there was, it is true, remarkably little of the random and vindictive killing that marked the European purges. But the battlefields of the war were, as we have noted, among the bloodiest the world had seen. The scorched earth policy of the Union armies, towards the end of the war, marked the beginning of what has since come to be called total war. The self-discipline of the American people, so praised by Professor Kristol in the Revolution, was much greater in the Civil War. But that is one of the reasons why that war was, in Churchill's phrase, fought out to the last inch.

In his insistent deradicalization of the American Revolution, Professor Kristol writes that

> the millenarian tradition in America long antedates the Revolution and is not intertwined with the idea of revolution itself. It was the Pilgrim Fathers, not the Founding Fathers, who first announced that this was God's country, that the American people had a divine mission to accomplish, that this people had been "chosen" to create some kind of model community for the rest of mankind.[11]

Certainly we cannot doubt that the Pilgrim Fathers had "announced" whatever it was that they did announce, before the Founding Fathers. After all, the two generations are separated by nearly a

55

century and a half. Between them there had been a great deal of persecution and bloody sectarian warfare in Europe, with reverberations in the New World (which is why the Pilgrims had come here.) Revulsion against this experience had combined with the powerful currents of secular thought in the Enlightenment to cause a great transformation in the idea of the proper role of religion in human life altogether, and in political life in particular. It is doubtful whether the Pilgrim Fathers would have understood the modern concept of the separation of church and state, and more doubtful that they would have approved of it. By 1776 the way was largely prepared for such a separation here, a separation which soon became a hallmark of American constitutionalism. Of the three things Jefferson wished to be inscribed on his tombstone, the first was that he was author of the Declaration of Independence, and the second that he was author of the Virginia Statute of Religious Freedom. Third, of course, was that he was Father of the University of Virginia. A *secularized* version of the old religious millenarianism was however not merely intertwined with the idea of revolution, it was the very essence of that idea. Professor Kristol admits that

> one can find a great many publicists during the Revolution who insisted that, with the severance of ties from Britain, the colonies had reverted to a Lockean "state of nature" and were now free to create a new political order that would mark a new stage in human history. . . .[12]

While admitting that "such assertions were popular enough" Professor Kristol admonishes us that "it would be a mistake to take them too seriously." The reason he gives is

> that Americans had encountered their "state of nature" generations earlier and had made their "social compact" at that time. The primordial "social contract" was signed and sealed on the *Mayflower*—literally signed and sealed. The subsequent presence of all those signatures appended to the Declaration of Independence, beginning with John Hancock's, are but an echo of the original covenant.[13]

Now there is some difficulty in regarding the Mayflower Compact as "Lockean," since it was signed many years before John Locke was born. It was certainly an agreement constituting a civil polity. But its announced purposes—the glory of God, the advancement of the Christian faith, and the honor of King and country (the country being Great Britain, not the colony)—make it at least doubtful whether it was a polity such as John Locke would have thought fully merited the name. But be it as Lockean as Professor Kristol wishes, how in the world could it have been the primordial compact for the twelve colonies *other* than Massachusetts Bay? [It is even doubtful if the Mayflower Compact, which was for Plymouth Plantations, carried forward to Massachusetts.] In particular, how could it be the compact for Virginia, which was older than Plymouth? Moreover, it was the Virginia Company which provided the "patent" authorizing the Pilgrims to plant a colony "in the northern parts of Virginia."

But Professor Kristol has mistaken the application of the state of nature concept to the situation of the United Colonies, and the United States, in the Revolution. He seems to think that the state of nature (and the law of nature which governs it) is something men leave behind them, once and for all, when they enter (or consent to) civil society; or, alternatively, that it recurs only with the dissolution of civil society. But the case is far otherwise. The state of nature may recur within civil society, whenever the executive power (that is, police power) of that society is unable to extend its protection. Whenever that happens, the exercise of the executive power of the law of nature may be resumed. This was, for example, happening constantly upon the colonial frontiers, as it does today within our crime–ridden cities. All independent states or sovereigns are always in a state of nature, one with another. The state of *war*, according to Locke, occurs whenever there is a resort to *force without right*. And the state of war may arise *either* in civil society *or* within the state of nature. But whenever anyone—either a single individual, or a whole people—is subjected to force without right—recourse may be made, without any limitation, to the laws of nature. The Declaration of Independence asserted that the government of Great Britain had evinced a design to reduce the colonies under absolute despotism, which means a condition in which they might be subject to unlimited force without right. Hence the former colonies were, with respect to Great Britain, in a state of nature which was also a state of war. Hence they were perfectly free, under the laws of nature, to provide new guards for their future safety, and to institute new government. The laws of nature which govern the state of

57

nature provided direct and immediate authority to the signatories of the Declaration, and the people they represented, without any reference whatever, to the Mayflower or any other compact, real or imagined. Those signatures were then no such "echo" as Professor Kristol imagines. The Signers acted under what Madison, in the forty–third number of *The Federalist*, called "the great principle of self-preservation . . . the transcendent law of natural and of nature's God."[14]

The right of freedom of the newly independent United States "to create a new political order that would mark a new stage in human history" was then not in the least affected by whether or not the social compacts uniting the former colonists with each other had or had not been dissolved and re-constituted in the course of the Revolution. Nevertheless, the question was discussed. According to James Madison

> . . . [it] was brought before Congress at its first session [under the Constitution] by Doctor Ramsay, who contested the election of William Smith; who though born in South Carolina, had been absent at the date of independence. The decision was, that his birth in the Colony made him a member of society in its new as well as its original state.[15]

By deciding that William Smith did not have to be "naturalized" the Congress decided in effect that there had been no dissolution of civil society because of the Revolution. Nevertheless, they distinguished the "new" from the "original" state. And in that new state, the American people enjoyed a freedom they had not enjoyed before, to institute new government, such as to them should seem "most likely to effect their safety and happiness." Professor Kristol says at one point that the purpose of the Revolution "was to bring our political institutions into a more perfect correspondence with an actual 'American way of life' which no one even dreamed of challenging."[16] This statement I find impossible to reconcile with the struggle in which both Jefferson and Madison engaged, both for religious disestablishment, and for the abolition of primogeniture an entail. That struggle was for a way of life unknown to eighteenth century Britain, as it was to the world. The commitment to a regime of civil and religious liberty resulting from the American Revolution was radical; indeed, it represented the most radical break with the past ever made in human history.

That the American people had a divine mission to perform, not for themselves alone, but for all mankind, is implied if not expressed in all the great documents of the Revolution, and of the American political tradition. This mission is given, not primarily by the God of the Old or New Testaments, but by the God of nature, who speaks through man's unassisted reason. Here is the young Alexander Hamilton, during the Revolution, giving expression to this new, secularized version of the old theological doctrine of direct inspiration.

> The sacred rights of mankind are not to be rummaged for among old parchments or musty records [not even old social compacts!]. They are written, as with a sunbeam, in the whole volume of human nature, *by the hand of divinity itself*, and can never be erased or obscured by mortal power [Emphasis added].[17]

By virtue of the proposition that all men are created equal, this nation became the first in the history of the world to enter upon the stage of independent existence, claiming independence, not in virtue of its own particular qualities, but in virtue of rights which it shared with all men everywhere. The American people, by being the first to announce these universal rights, made their experiment in free government the testing ground for all. In that sense, they did indeed become a "chosen" people who, if they succeeded, would surely "make a new beginning for all mankind" that would "mark a new stage in human history."

Professor Kristol declares at one point that "The most fascinating aspect of the American Revolution is the severe way it kept questioning itself about the meaning of what is was doing." "Enthusiasm there certainly was," he concedes, ". . . but this enthusiasm was tempered by doubt, introspection, anxiety, skepticism."[18]

I would surely like to see the documents in which "the American Revolution . . . kept questioning itself," since I have never encountered any and wonder why Professor Kristol does not cite them. A revolution centered upon truths declared to be self-evident, truths written by the hand of divinity itself, never to be erased or obscured by mortal power, hardly seems like a revolution beset by doubt, introspection, or skepticism as to its *meaning*. Anxiety there certainly was, but anxiety for the *outcome*, not for the truth, justice, or millenarian significance of the Revolution itself. Professor Kristol, it seems to me, has confused the cautious and prudent temper in which the business of the Revolution was conducted, with the boundless confidence of its votaries in the beneficent power of its principles to transform the political life of man on earth.

The Declaration, by proclaiming the *unity* of the human race, and the *universality* of its rights, constituted an epoch in secular history as significant and as unique, as that in sacred history, that followed the proclamation upon Sinai of the *unity* and *universality* of the living God. Moreover, one cannot forbear pointing out that Moses, in his dealings with the God of Israel, seemed to show far more doubt, introspection, and skepticism, than ever Jefferson and his cohorts did, in their transactions on behalf of the God of nature!

Professor Kristol also speaks of the Declaration as "calm" and "legalistic". I had thought it notable for its burning eloquence. Abraham Lincoln praised Jefferson above all for introducing into a "merely revolutionary document, an abstract truth, applicable to all men and all times."[19] Not what justified the American people legalistically, but what justified all peoples everywhere politically, in their struggle not only for independence, but for self-government, is what commended the Declaration to Lincoln. The pronouncement of that "abstract truth" transformed the struggle of a single people at a given moment, into an unending world struggle against tyranny. So Jefferson thought nearly a half century after penning his immortal words. The following is from a message he wrote for the festivities on the fiftieth anniversary of independence, the day that he and John Adams were to undergo their apotheosis.

> May it [the Declaration] be to the world what I believe it will be (to some parts sooner, to others later, but finally to all) the signal of arousing men to burst the chains, under which monkish ignorance and superstition had persuaded them to bind themselves, and to assume the blessings and security of self-government.[20]

In Independence Hall, in February, 1861, on his way to Washington to assume the presidency of an already divided nation, Lincoln asked "what great principle or idea it was that [had] kept this Confederacy so long together."

> It was not the mere matter of the separation of the colonies from the mother land; but something in that Declaration giving liberty, not alone to the

> people of this country, but hope to the world for all future time. It was that
> which gave promise that in due time the weights would be lifted from the
> shoulders of all men, and that *all* should have an equal chance [Emphasis in
> the original].[21]

"Hope to the world for all future time" is millenarian rhetoric that is
more than intertwined with the idea of the Revolution.

In speaking of lifting the weights from the shoulders of all men,
Lincoln was moreover evoking a figure of speech intensely familiar
in his America, as it had been to his colonial ancestors. In John
Bunyan's *Pilgrim's Progress*, Christian's journey in quest of salvation
is represented as that of a man seeking relief from the terrible
weight of a burden strapped to his back that he cannot put down.
The burden of course symbolizes original sin. In Lincoln's speech,
original sin becomes inequality, and the release of the world from
the burden of inequality becomes the secular—and political—
equivalent of the release of the world from sin. In Jefferson's and
Lincoln's understanding of the American Revolution, the mission of
that Revolution, in saving the world, was no less universalistic or
messianic than that of Christianity. In 1848, Lincoln had declared in
Congress that

> Any people anywhere, being inclined and having the power, have the *right*
> to rise up and shake off the existing government, and form a new one that
> suits them better. This is a most valuable, a most sacred right—a right which,
> we hope and believe, is to liberate the world.[22]

It was not long after the speech in Independence Hall that Father
Abraham's armies were marching to the Battle Hymn of the
Republic, and singing "As he died to make men holy let us die to
make men free." The assimilation of the older religious millenarianism into the Revolutionary political creed was perfect and complete.

Alexander Hamilton, in the first number of *The Federalist*,
wrote that

> It has been frequently remarked that it seems to have been reserved to the
> people of this country, by their conduct and example, to decide the important
> question, whether societies of men are really capable or not of establishing
> good government from reflection and choice, or whether they are forever
> destined to depend for their political constitutions on accident and force.[23]

Hamilton says that it was "frequently remarked" that this nation was to decide whether or nor mankind would "forever" depend upon accident and force for their governments. No doubt those who did so remark were the "great many publicists" whom Professor Kristol invites us not to take too seriously. But Hamilton took them seriously enough to regard their opinion as perhaps the most important ground upon which the American people ought to be persuaded to adopt the Constitution. When Lincoln at Gettysburg spoke of the Civil War as a test, whether this nation, or any nation, founded upon the principles of the Declaration of Independence could long endure, he was echoing Hamilton in the opening number of *The Federalist*. The messianic theme is then an everpresent element in the teachings of the soberest statesmen of the American political tradition.

In the tenth chapter of the Gospel according to Matthew, Jesus says that he has come to bring, not peace, but a sword; that he has come to set the son against the father, and the daughter against the mother; and that a man's foes will be those of his own household. The culminating event of the American Revolution is the American Civil War, the most poignant and pathetic event of modern history. Above all others, it was a brothers' war. In no other comparable conflict—not even the French and Russian revolutions—have households been so rent asunder. The doctrine of equality, like that of divine love, seems also to have brought not peace but a sword.

The fundamental cause of the American Civil War was not slavery as such. It was slavery in a nation *dedicated to the proposition that all men are created equal.* From the moment of that dedication, slavery as a permanent and hereditary condition of any class of human beings within the American polity became an unbearable anomaly. It is Professor Kristol's thesis that the Founding Fathers at the end of their days looked back in satisfied tranquillity at what they had wrought. Had they done so, they must have been blind to the bitter strife of the political factions around them; and they would have been open to the charge—which has often been wrongly made—that they were morally insensitive to the demands of their own principles. The truth is that they were far less successful statesmen than Professor Kristol says they were. But they were much greater, and much more interesting men, than they would have been, had they been successful in the way he describes.

Professor Kristol's revision of American history is reminiscent of the eighteenth century revisers of Shakespeare who, among other "improvements," provided a happy ending for *King Lear*.

Professor Kristol denies that, after the Revolution, the political thought of the Founding Fathers was "seriously studied." In fact, it was not merely studied, but constantly ransacked by both sides in all the great debates. Lincoln began his Cooper Institute address, in February, 1860, as follows.

> In his speech last autumn, at Columbus, Ohio, as reported in "The New York Times," Senator Douglas said:
> "*Our fathers, when they framed the government under which we live, understood this question just as well, and even better, than we do now.*"
> I fully endorse this, and I adopt it as a text for this discourse. I so adopt it because it furnishes a precise and an agreed starting point for a discussion between Republicans and that wing of the Democracy headed by Senator Douglas. It simply leaves the inquiry: "*What was the understanding those fathers had of the question mentioned?*"[24]

In beginning his Cooper Institute speech thus—a speech marked by profound research in documentary sources—Lincoln was only following the tradition of debate that had dominated American politics in his lifetime. But Professor Kristol thinks that in this same period, "political theory lost its vigor." This is hard to reconcile with the dominating presence in such times of men like John Quincy Adams, Daniel Webster, John C. Calhoun, and Abraham Lincoln. Professor Kristol laments the lack of serious study of *The Federalist*. That work was, of course, constantly cited in the debates of the ante-bellum period. I suspect that it has, in recent years, been more seriously studied than Professor Kristol thinks. Charles A. Beard devoted one of his last books, *The Republic*, to celebrating its virtues along with those of the Constitution. In the course of that celebration, Beard seemed to retract most of what he had written earlier in depreciation of those documents. But it detracts nothing from the genius of *The Federalist*, to suggest that another book, *The Political Debates of Abraham Lincoln and Stephen A. Douglas*, reveals the inner tension of the polity that emerged from the Revolution, and hence the inner character of the Revolution, even more profoundly than the earlier work.

Thomas Jefferson is the dominating figure in the articulation of the American cause in the Revolution. *A Summary View of the Rights of British America* is the basic source from which the position of the Continental Congress was derived, up to and including the Declaration of Independence. That Jefferson was generally more radical than his countrymen is true, but he generally managed to bring them up to his mark in time. On the question of slavery, however, it appears that he at first half succeeded, and then completely failed. That the principles of the Revolution condemned slavery, however, was simply axiomatic, for Jefferson himself. Here he is, in the *Summary View*, addressing the King:

> The abolition of domestic slavery is the great object of desire in those colonies where it was, unhappily, introduced in their infant state. But previous to the enfranchisement of the slaves we have, it is necessary to exclude all further importations from Africa. Yet our repeated attempts to effect this . . . [have] been hitherto defeated by his Majesty's negative: thus preferring the immediate advantages of a few British corsairs, to the lasting interests of the American states, and to the rights of human nature, deeply wounded by this infamous practice.[25]

It is well known that, in his original draft of the Declaration, Jefferson denounced the King for having "waged cruel war against human nature itself, violating its most sacred rights of life and liberty in the persons of a distant people who never offended him. . . ."[26] This denunciation is explicitly directed only at the slave trade as such. But in the *Summary View* the exclusion of further importations is mentioned as the necessary preliminary to "the abolition of domestic slavery" by "enfranchisement of the slaves we have."

No more remarkable indictment of slavery was ever penned than that found in Jefferson's *Notes on Virginia* written while the Revolution was still in progress. The following is from the Eighteenth Query.

> The whole commerce between master and slave is a perpetual exercise of the most boisterous passions, the most unremitting despotism on the one part, and degrading submissions on the other. . . . The man must be a prodigy who can retain his manners and morals undepraved by such circumstances. And with what execrations should the statesman be loaded, who, permitting one half the citizens to trample the other, transforms these into despots, and these into enemies. . . .[27]

Although this passage has been frequently quoted, sufficient note has not been taken of the extraordinary characterization of the slaves as "one half the citizens." Jefferson knew perfectly well that the concept "slave" excludes by definition that of "citizen," and *vice versa*. But the sentence containing this solecism elucidates it. Slavery, he says, makes men enemies; that is, it alienates them from one another. It destroys the bonds which *should* link them in mutual regard for their rights as men, and make it possible for them to become fellow-citizens. A collection of despots does not make a free people, any more than a free people will be ruled by a despot. Jefferson will not only not let his countrymen forget that the slaves possess the same unalienable rights that they do, but he insists that their own freedom depends, in the last analysis, upon the recognition of the rights of the slaves. The following is a passage which Abraham Lincoln would quote over and over again. Nothing could be clearer than that Jefferson believed, in the midst of the Revolution, that the problem of Negro slavery had to be solved by the new republic, and that if it was not solved, the Revolution would be a failure.

> And can the liberties of a nation be thought secure when we have removed their *only firm basis*, a conviction in the minds of the people that these liberties are the gift of God? That they are not to be violated but with his wrath? Indeed, I tremble for my country when I reflect that God is just; that his justice cannot sleep forever . . . [Emphasis added].[28]

Jefferson then considered that a civil and servile war might not only be possible, but "that it may become probable by supernatural interference!"

> The Almighty has no attribute which can take side with us in such a contest.[29]

Who cannot see the influence of this upon Lincoln's second inaugural address, wherein the Civil War is regarded as a divine scourge for the offense of slavery? In so regarding it, Lincoln asks, echoing Jefferson, whether we shall "discern . . . any departure from those divine attributes which the believers in a living God always ascribe to Him?"[30]

Jefferson ends the Eighteenth Query with some optimism. He thinks that, since the beginning of the Revolution, and in harmony with it, "The spirit of the master is abating, that of the slave rising from the dust, his condition mollifying, the way I hope preparing, under the auspices of heaven, *for a total emancipation* . . . [Emphasis added]."[31] But Jefferson should have been warned by the circumstances that caused the committee to strike the passage against the slave trade from his draft of the Declaration, that those who had an economic interest in slavery, could not be easily led to see it as wrong. The following is from a letter Jefferson wrote only four years after the *Notes on Virginia*.

> What a stupendous, what an incomprehensible machine is man! who can endure toil, famine, stripes, imprisonment, and death itself, in vindication of his own liberty, and, the next moment, be deaf to all those motives whose power supported him through his trial, and inflict on his fellow man a bondage, *one hour of which is fraught with more misery than ages of that which he rose in rebellion to oppose* [Emphasis added].[32]

These powerful lines, are as revealing as anything ever written, of the inner conflict which the Revolution, far from resolving, only unleashed upon the American people and the world. By the time of the Missouri crisis, in 1820, any hope that Jefferson might have had that the slavery question might be solved, without disunion and without war, seems to have been gone. ". . . this momentous question," he then wrote,

> like a fire-bell in the night, awakened and filled me with terror. I considered it at once as the knell of the Union. It is hushed indeed for the moment. But this is a reprieve only. . . . I regret that I am now to die in the belief that the useless sacrifices of themselves by the generation of 1776, to acquire self-government and happiness to their country, is to be thrown away . . . and my only consolation . . . that I shall not live to weep over it. . . .[33]

In a message to Congress in Special Session, July 4, 1861, Abraham Lincoln declared that the leaders of the South knew that

> they could never raise their treason to any respectable magnitude by any name which implies violation of law. . . . Accordingly, [Lincoln continued,] they commenced by an insidious debauching of the public mind. They invented an ingenious sophism, which, if conceded, was followed by perfectly logical steps . . . to the complete destruction of the Union. The sophism is, that any State of the Union may, *consistently* with the national Constitution, and therefore *lawfully* and *peacefully*, withdraw from the Union without the consent of the Union or of any other State. . . . With rebellion thus sugar-coated they have been drugging the public mind of their section for more than thirty years . . . [Emphasis in original].[34]

Lincoln's chronology of "more than thirty years" places the origin of the conspiracy to destroy the Union during the nullification crisis. That crisis ended in one of the famous compromises of the ante–bellum period. South Carolina believed it had successfully compelled a downward revision of the "tariff of abominations," and had repealed its Ordinance of Secession only after tariff revision was assured. The nationalists could point to the fact that the Force Act had been repealed only after the Ordinance, and that all the while the duties had been collected. From a longer perspective it can be seen that the confrontation between South Carolina and the Union was in no wise resolved in 1832, but only postponed until 1860. Then it was renewed in a far deadlier manner. Lincoln was surely right in saying in effect that the "ingenious sophism" had been planted in the public mind of the South by the nullifiers. He might have noted that the equal and opposite principle—the constitutional right of the Union to coerce a nullifying or seceding state—had also been planted in the public mind outside the South, about the same time, by the redoubtable Andrew Jackson, whose precedents Lincoln was closely to follow.

In maintaining that the "ingenious sophism" had been "invented" during the nullification controversy, Lincoln was implicitly denying the South Carolina claim that all its principles had been derived from the Kentucky and Virginia Resolutions of 1798, and from the Kentucky Resolutions of 1799, as well as from Madison's Report of 1800. But before Lincoln, Madison himself, in 1830, had *explicitly* denied the authority claimed by South Carolina's spokesmen from his earlier pronouncements. Madison's role in the nullification controversy remains one of the largely untold stories in American history. One reason for this, is the great disparity in theoretical competence, between most of the scholars who have attempted to tell it, and the principals in the controversy. The two profoundest antagonists then were John C. Calhoun and James Madison, who must certainly rank among the most acute political controversialists the world has ever seen.

Senator Hayne of South Carolina sent a copy of his speech in reply to Daniel Webster to Madison. Since the speech quoted copiously from Madison's 1798–1800 writings against the Alien and

Sedition Acts, Hayne expected to have Madison's approval. What he received was exactly the opposite. Madison's reply to Hayne, somewhat refurbished, was incorporated in another letter, to Edward Everett. This was published by Everett in the October, 1830 issue of the *North American Review*. It was to be the only *public* statement by Madison on the entire nullification question. But his private statements, in letters, and in unpublished essays, constitute a considerable body of writing. Certainly the best of this writing ranks with the best of his earlier writing, including the great essays for *The Federalist*. That some of the rhetoric of the earlier Virginia and Kentucky Resolutions bore a certain resemblance to the later South Carolina doctrines, is undeniable. But resemblance is not identity. We might put the matter in theological terms, by saying that those who believe in many gods, and those who believe in one God, are all theists; and as such are to be distinguished from atheists. Madison contended from beginning to end, that his Virginia Resolutions sanctioned the interposition of the *states*, whereas South Carolina claimed the right of a single *state*, to arrest the action of an allegedly unconstitutional federal law. Madison further insisted that such interposition of the states as he had envisioned, was nothing more than the exercise of the states' constituent function, as prescribed in the amending clauses of the Constitution itself. But there was no textual foundation whatever for nullification in the South Carolina sense. As to the sanction claimed from the Kentucky Resolutions—which Madison conceded were less guarded in their language than Virginia's—Madison noted that what Jefferson referred to as a *natural* right, South Carolina claimed as a *constitutional* right.

Despite Madison's vigorous arguments in the *North American Review*, and despite the obvious inspiration he lent to a number of other speakers in the public arena, the Carolinians stubbornly paraded his earlier pronouncements. On one occasion, the Nullifying Convention in one of its major addresses attempted publicly to rebuke and rebut the contemporaneous James Madison with the former James Madison. In one of history's amazing ironies, we may say that it anticipated in principle the poetry of Dostoievski's Grand Inquisitor, by denying the living witness of the Father of the Constitution, in the name of what it claimed to be his own original Gospel.

In my essay "Partly Federal, Partly National,"[35] I have pointed to the comparative success of South Carolina, in the court of present day historiography, in its claim to the authority of the Kentucky and Virginia Resolutions for the principles of its doctrines. Certainly Madison himself viewed with melancholy foreboding, the results of the nullification crisis. In it, moreover, he must have seen the fatal exception his own argument in the *Federalist* had provided, against the success of the system. In the famous number fifty–one, Madison had written that, in the extended republic of the United States, there would be such a "great variety of intersts, parties, and sects . . . [that] a coalition of a majority of the whose society could *seldom* take place on any other principles than those of justice and the general good [Emphasis added]."[36] But such a coalition need not take place *often*, to undo the structure of the whole. Calhoun's amazingly shrewd argument, in the South Carolina Exposition and Protest, was directed precisely to the argument of the fifty–first *Federalist*, and purported to show that exactly such an unjust coalition of a majority as Madison had said would *seldom* occur, had in fact occurred in the passage of the tariff of abominations. But both Madison and Calhoun knew, that it was not the tariff as such, which was at the bottom of the difficulty. It was the threat of a federal surplus which might arise from the collection of the tariff, and the possibility that that surplus might be put to work to finance a plan for the compensated emancipation of slaves, such a plan as Jefferson, Madison, and Monroe had all, in principle, endorsed. Madison, like Jefferson, knew from the beginning that the extended republic would endure, only if it had at its common foundation, those principles of the Enlightenment which were supremely expressed in the Declaration of Independence, the principles of the Revolution, rightly understood. The Republic would endure, and the prudential arguments of the *Federalist* would prove prophetic, only if the proposition that slavery was a violation of the rights of human nature did not come into fundamental contention. But the nullification crisis was followed almost without intermission, by the rise of radical abolitionism, on the one hand, and by the rise of the positive good school of slavery, on the other. As I have argued in my previous essay, Madison's constitutional doctrines—"partly national, partly federal" as distinguished from the wholly national school—were inherited by Abraham Lincoln. But in Lincoln they were united with that policy and that program which alone could make them viable: the policy and program which made the defense of constitutionalism contingent upon the condemnation of slavery.

When Madison died in 1836, he left a final "Advice to My Country," advice which, he said, "may be considered as issuing from the tomb." "The advice nearest to my heart," he declared

> and deepest in my convictions is that the Union of the States be cherished and perpetuated. Let the open enemy to it be regarded as a Pandora with her box opened: and the disguised one, as the Serpent creeping with his deadly wiles into Paradise.[37]

But Madison knew that the great danger to the Union would always come from those who would profess the highest devotion to it, until the end. He also knew that the Serpent had already entered Paradise, and that he himself had unwittingly helped to leave the gates of the garden ajar. His own labors, together with those of Andrew Jackson, and the other anti-nullifiers, had only "scotched the snake, not killed it." And Madison, like all his countrymen, was too good a student of the Bible not to know that once the Serpent enters Paradise, the fate of its inhabitants is already determined. So much for Professor Kristol's thesis of the tranquil repose of the Founding Fathers.

Near the beginning of his Distinguished Lecture, Professor Kristol undertakes to instruct us in the duties of patriotic piety.

> We are arrogant and condescending towards all ancestors, because we are so convinced we understand them better than they understood themselves— whereas piety assumes that they still understood us better than we understand ourselves.[38]

Surely it is a duty of scholarly objectivity to try to understand the statesmen and thinkers of the past—not only ancestors—as they understood themselves, before trying to understand them differently or better. This is not merely a dictate of humility or even of common sense. It is a matter of logical necessity. To understand someone better than he understood himself implies that one has first understood him *as* he understood himself. One cannot evaluate the self-understanding of another, without first showing that one knows what it is. But Professor Kristol's piety seems to be something other than this axiom of scholarship. It appears to involve that "willing suspension of disbelief" that accompanies both poetic and religious faith. He seems to invert chronology and common sense in telling us what piety assumes about ancestors. Are they Homeric gods, who enjoy immortality in this world? When was it that they began to understand us better than we understand ourselves, since they "still" do?

But I find no evidence that Professor Kristol attempts to understand the Revolutionary "ancestors" *as* they understood themselves. Whenever he finds them saying things that do not fit his preconceptions he advises us, as we have already seen, not to take it too seriously. At one point he is obliged to admit that the men of the Revolution "frequently expressed [themselves] enthusiastically, in a kind of messianic rhetoric." But he then hastens to add that "most of them, most of the time—did not permit themselves to become bewitched by that rhetoric."[39] Thus by his own testimony, these "ancestors" gave *frequent, enthusiastic,* and *messianic* speeches. Yet Professor Kristol assures us, in virtue of his science of hermeneutics, the mysteries of which he does not divulge—but which we may in this case describe as a bewitch hunt—that "most of them, most of the time" didn't really mean what they said. Yet we, in all piety, must ask, how does he know?

In another place, Professor Kristol writes that, "To perceive the true purposes of the American Revolution, it is wise to ignore some of the more grandiloquent declamations of the moment. . . ."[40] As nearly as I can tell, Professor Kristol has ignored not some, but *all* the grandiloquent declamations of the Revolution. The most grandiloquent of all, of course, is to be found in the Declaration of Independence. What Abraham Lincoln called "that immortal emblem of humanity," Professor Kristol has called that "calm, legalistic document." The true spirit of the Revolution, says Professor Kristol, is to be found in "the kinds of political activity the Revolution unleashed."

This, in turn, is to be found, "above all," in "constitution-making," particularly in the states. Yet to read Professor Kristol, one would never guess that seven of the original state constitutions were prefaced by bills of rights. These were not, as in the later federal constitution, legal rights, or legal limitations upon governmental power. They were statements of principle exactly like that which stands at the front of the Declaration of Independence. They were less succinct and less eloquent than Jefferson's, but they were not a bit less universalistic as statements of the principles underlying *all* government, and hence no less grandiloquent. What Professor Kristol does not seem to understand, is that "the more grandiloquent declamations of the moment" are precisely the places in which to look for the self-understanding of the Revolutionary ancestors. It was just such declamations whch transformed them from grumbling Englishmen into flaming American patriots. Jefferson himself, many years later, said that the Declaration was intended to be an expression of "the American mind." What Jefferson did was to transform the most widely and deeply felt convictions into a concentrated, articulate, and flaming faith. Grandiloquent declamations are what the Revolutionary ancestors hungered for, and because they did, their generation produced more of them than any before and, perhaps, any since.

Professor Kristol's Distinguished Lecture on the American Revolution is above all an invitation to ignore Thomas Jefferson, who was certainly the principal source of all those "grandiloquent declamations." But Professor Kristol cannot quite bring himself to say this. Instead, he tells us that "Tom Paine, an English radical who never really understood America, is especially worth ignoring."[41] Let us then conclude with a few words about Tom Paine.

Paine's career went through different phases. His patronage of the French Revolution in its earlier phases was not very different from Jefferson's. His enthusiasm however was not as well governed by tact. But whatever Paine did *after* the American Revolution must not obscure our vision of his enormous contributions to the cause of American Independence. Paine was one of the most gifted political writers who ever lived. One can perhaps best describe his role to a twentieth century audience by saying that *Common Sense* and *The Crisis* did for the turning points of the American Revolution what Churchill's speeches did to rally Britain, in the dark days after Dunkirk. Professor Kristol no doubt regards him as a vulgar fellow. But Paine's "vulgarity," such as it was, gave him an ability to talk to the common man in accents they understood. None of the colonial leaders—certainly not George Washington, and probably not even Jefferson—even with the advantages of their official positions, could rouse the masses of men as could Paine. It is well to keep in mind that, by a general estimate of present–day scholars, the American public, on the eve of independence, was about one–third favorable, one–third hostile, and one–third neutral or indifferent. It was the *intensity* of the patriot feelings that carried the day, and Paine's contribution to this intensity was incalculable. We quote from John Richard Alden's *The American Revolution*:

> Chiefly influential in leading patriots toward formal separation was Thomas Paine, whose *Common Sense* came anonymously from the press in January, 1776. . . . A gifted writer and propagandist, he now burst like a meteor into the arena of public affairs. In phrases at once eloquent and passionate, Paine denounced the masters of his native country and pleaded for an American proclamation of independence . . . *Common Sense* had an enormous circulation, 120,000 copies being printed within three months . . . and it has been described not infrequently as the determining factor in the debate over independence.[42]

In a footnote, Professor Alden cites Paine's biographer, Moncure Conway, as asserting that "almost a half a million copies [of *Common Sense*] were sold soon after publication."[43] In a nation of four millions, this would be the equivalent of a sale of twenty–five millions today. But since there was no competing form of communication, in either radio, television, or moving pictures, the concentrated effect was much greater. It is likely that every literate American read the forty–seven page booklet, and that many of those who could not read heard it read.

Not less impressive is *The Crisis*. The first issue of this pamphlet was in December, 1776, six months after the Declaration, and when the warm enthusiasm of July was confronted with the cold reality of a long, hard war. Think what such words as these must have meant to the men in the ranks of Washington's army.

> These are the times that try men's souls: The summer soldier and the sunshine patriot will, in this crisis, shrink from the service of his country; but

he that stands it NOW deserves the love and thanks of man and woman. Tyranny, like hell, is not easily conquered; yet we have this consolation with us, that the harder the conflict the more glorious the triumph.[44]

There is a tradition of fighting oratory in the English–speaking peoples, that encompasses Queen Elizabeth I's address to her troops at Tilbury, on the eve of the Spanish Armada, a tradition that includes the poetry of Shakespeare in his character of Henry V, addressing his troops on St. Crispin's day, before Agincourt, a tradition that runs like a bright thread through the Gettysburg Address to Churchill's appeal to Britain, to make this their "finest hour." In Tom Paine—who did not himself disdain to carry a musket in the ranks of the Continentals—speaks the spirit of Valley Forge. And in this great tradition of English oratory, he bears a most honored place. It would be a travesty of the Bicentennial to ignore him.

After the American Revolution, and after partisan politics in the United States became embittered by the issues of the French Revolution, Paine—an intense Francophile—became intensely controversial. The story of Paine's relationship to Jefferson is long and complicated. There is no question but that, at some time or another, they were very close. There is much dispute over whether many of Jefferson's most notable pronouncements—including even the phraseology of the Declaration—did not originate with Paine. The least that one can say is, that if Paine did not prompt Jefferson to express certain famous thoughts, then Jefferson must have prompted Paine. When Jefferson became President, the mercurial Paine became something of a political embarrassment to him, and Jefferson eventually kept his distance. But there is no evidence that Jefferson ever regarded Paine as less than an authoritative expounder of the ideas they held in common. Jefferson himself never produced an orderly and systematic work of political theory, nor did any other native born American of his generation. *The Rights of Man* is virtually the only, as it is the clearest and most comprehensive statement of radical republican thought in Revolutionary America. When it was first published in the United States, it appeared with an endorsement by Jefferson. Jefferson later said that he had not intended his endorsement for publication. But when he was subjected to political attack along with Paine because of it, Jefferson calmly declared that such an attack was justified, "for I profess the same principles."

The importance of *The Rights of Man* is not limited to the era of the Revolution. For example, we give part of Abraham Lincoln's reply to Douglas and Taney, in the wake of the Dred Scott decision in 1857. The latter agreed in maintaining that the Signers of the Declaration, in affirming the equality of all men, were in fact affirming only the equality of British subjects of this continent with British subjects born and residing in Great Britain. "I had thought," said Lincoln,

> the Declaration promised something better than the condition of British subjects; but no, it only meant that we should be *equal* to them in their own oppressed and *unequal* condition. According to that, it gave no promise that having kicked off the King and Lords of Great Britain, we should not at once be saddled with a King and Lords of our own. [45]

Here is the very breath of Tom Paine, speaking with the voice of Abraham Lincoln. We would add that Mark Twain's enormously popular *Connecticut Yankee in King Arthur's Court* is little more than a novelistic version of themes drawn from the *Rights of Man* and the *Age of Reason*. Because of his attack on Biblical religion in the latter work, Paine has never been entirely respectable with American conservatives, since the days of Fisher Ames. But that latter worthy did not think much worse of Paine than of his friend Jefferson, who had written, "it does me no injury for my neighbor to say there are twenty gods, or no God. It neither picks my pocket nor breaks my leg." [46] It was as unjust and unworthy of Theodore Roosevelt to call him a "dirty little atheist," as it is of Professor Kristol, to invite us to ignore him.

Professor Diamond's Distinguished Lecture occupies what must, from every point of view, be considered the post of honor in the Bicentennial Series. It is the only one that was delivered in Independence Square. Congress Hall, the site of the lecture, is where the first United States Congresses under the Constitution met, from 1790 until 1800. It is but a short step across the Square to Independence Hall, where both the Declaration of Independence and the Constitution first saw the light of day. Far more important however is Professor Diamond's theme, which is the inner relationship between these famous documents. There can be little doubt—in my mind there is none at all—that upon this relationship turns the innermost meaning of the American Revolution, and of the American political tradition which it established.

Professor Diamond's thesis concerning this relationship is, in its way, boldly original. Notwithstanding his emphasis upon the modesty, sobriety, and coolness of his hero, James Madison, his thesis is uncompromisingly radical and extreme. The Declaration, he says, although "indispensable [as a] source of the feelings and sentiments of Americans and of the spirit of liberty in which their institutions were conceived . . . is devoid of guidance as to what those institutions should be."[47] Professor Diamond, we repeat, maintains that the Declaration of Independence is *devoid of guidance* as to what the political institutions should be under which the American (or any other) people ought to live.

At another point Professor Diamond asserts that "there is nothing in the Declaration which goes beyond the sentiment of liberty."[48] And at still another that "The Declaration . . . offers no guidance for the construction of free government and hence offers no aid in protecting the American form of free government under the Constitution."[49] And at yet another ". . . that the Declaration, while richly nurturing in humanity a love of free government . . . can offer no guidance whatsover . . . for the American democratic institutions which sprang from that love of freedom."[50]

If Professor Diamond had merely said that the Declaration had provided only the general principles for the construction of free government, but had left all the details—even the most important details—open, his thesis would have been a familiar one. But his absolute and uncompromising formulation of *no guidance*, a formulation that, like "all men are created equal," would be destroyed by a single exception, makes him a commentator as radical and novel as the event he celebrates.

"As to those democratic institutions" embodied in the Constitutions, he writes,

> the Declaration says no more than this: if you choose the democratic form of
> government, rather than the aristocratic or monarchic or any mixture thereof,

76

it must be a democratic government which secures to all people their unalienable rights. But how to do that? The Declaration is silent.[51]

And then Professor Diamond continues: "Indeed, this silence is the splendid distinction of the American Revolution. And it is the first evidence of the sobriety to which I allude in the title of this lecture."[52] The Declaration, we thus observe, not only offers *no guidance* in the construction of free government, but this very absence of guidance, this supposed silence, is the "splendid distinction of the American Revolution" and its "first evidence" of sobriety.

We must wonder however at how the Declaration can, as Professor Diamond insists that it does, uncompromisingly enjoin upon *all* governments the duty to secure the unalienable rights of *all* people, while supplying *no guidance* towards that end. This on the face of it seems most unreasonable. Surely, such a universal obligation must imply a universal criterion or standard of when unalienable rights *are* and when the *are not* being secured. How could the Signers declare a universal duty, without implying some correspondingly universal means of fulfilling it? And how could they omit indicating—if not expressly declaring—what those means were? What time or place could be more expedient or proper, than that afforded by the document which declared to all the world that *all* governments exist rightfully, only to secure the unalienable rights of *all* men?

But again, is it not strange that the Declaration should be thoroughly neutral towards all forms of government? Did the Signers believe that the business of securing unalienable rights is not in the least affected by whether the government doing it is democratic or monarchic or aristocratic? The words of Abraham Lincoln, which we quoted earlier, still ring in our ears: that the Declaration, having "kicked off the King and Lords of Great Britain" gave promise that "we should not . . . be saddled with a King and Lords of our own." Professor Diamond would, no doubt, have called to Lincoln's attention the prohibition of titles of nobility in Section 9 of Article I of the Constitution as the guarantee against being saddled with a King and Lords, along with the guarantee of a republican form of government in Section 4 of Article IV. But Lincoln evidently regarded these as mere by-products of the Declaration of Independence. Professor

Diamond, in the course of his Distinguished Lecture, quoted with what appears to be complete approval, Lincoln's assertion that by the Declaration promise was given "that in due time the weights would be lifted from the shoulders of all men, and that *all* should have an equal chance." Does Professor Diamond think, or does he think that Lincoln thought, that monarchies and aristocracies—or even mixed regimes—provide the same "equal chance" as well–constructed democratic republics? It is one thing to say that well–constructed democratic republics are not always and everywhere possible. One can even say that the forms that give substance to the excellence of democratic republics may vary with circumstances and hence need not be always and everywhere precisely the same. But it is entirely different to say that the Declaration is simply neutral to all forms as such, and that it supplies no criteria for distinguishing in any way the instrinsic merits of the different forms of government.

But finally we come to the lamentable fact that the one injunction which, according to Professor Diamond, was unquestionably laid upon the Founding Fathers by the Declaration of Independence, is the one that they unquestionably did not obey. Whatever the Founding Fathers *did* do, they *did not* "secure to all people" their unalienable rights. Not only did the Constitution provide a guarantee to slavery in whatever states chose to have it (a guarantee which, incidentally, was absent from the Articles of Confederation), but it prohibited the United States from interfering in any way with the African slave trade, for at least twenty years. The Constitution thus guaranteed that the United States would continue to do, for at least twenty years, what Jefferson had bitterly denounced the King of Great Britain for doing, both in his *Summary View*, and in his draft of the Declaration, namely, "waging cruel war against human nature itself. . . ."

The failure of the Constitutional Convention to prohibit—or even to permit the prohibition of—the foreign slave trade, was a failure of incalculable magnitude. This trade was far from moribund. In the twenty year period during which the foreign slave trade continued under the Constitution, imports of slaves from Africa reached unprecedented highs. According to Fogel and Engerman "about as many Africans [were] brought into the United States during the thirty years from 1780 to 1810 as during the previous hundred and sixty years. . . ."[53] An examination of the curve of Fogel and Engelman's chart of slave imports, suggests that perhaps 90% of the slaves imported during that *thirty* years, came in during the *twenty* years that the Constitution gave this guarantee to piracy.

Professor Diamond's view of the making of the Constitution is unduly limited to the work of the Philadelphia Convention. It is no diminution of the stature of that ever–glorious—but still human— body, to suggest that the living Constitution generated in that period included at least two other notable documents. One was the Bill of Rights, added by the first Congress also under the tutelage of James Madison. The other was the Northwest Ordinance. This constitutional document is seldom given the attention by scholars and teachers that it deserves. Yet it did more to determine the shape of our westward expansion—which dominated the first century of our history—than did the Philadelphia Constitution. Its importance as one of our fundamental political arrangements is incalculable. It was the Northwest Ordinance which assured that the United States would in fact become in the full sense the "extended republic" celebrated in *The Federalist.* And it was the "extended republic" hypothesis of *The Federalist* which supplied the premise upon which the most powerful and famous defense of the Constitution rested.

What the Northwest Ordinance did, was to assure that the United States, in the course of the continental expansion which had already begun, would become a democratic, and not an autocratic republic. It did this in the following way:

1. By assuring that the territories of the United States would remain part of the United States; and that the citizens of the territories would be citizens of the United States.

2. By assuring that the territories, even before becoming states, would be governed by the same principles of civil and religious liberty as "form[ed] the basis whereon [the original thirteen] republics, their laws and constitutions, are erected."

3. By assuring that when any territory possessed enough inhabitants to become a state, it would be admitted upon a basis of full political equality with the original thirteen.

4. By declaring that "Religion, morality, and knowledge, being necessary to good government and the happiness of mankind, schools and the means of education shall forever be encouraged."

5. By declaring that "There shall be neither slavery nor involuntary servitude in the said territory, otherwise than in the punishment of crimes. . . ."

By linking of the themes of civil and religious liberty, the republican form of government, the encouragement of education, and the prohibition of slavery, the Northwest Ordinance is of priceless import. It fulfills a function in the founding achieved neither by the Declaration or the Constitution, in isolation from it. The Ordinance was actually drafted by Nathan Dane of Massachusetts, but Dane's text derives its major features from Jefferson's draft of three years before. Jefferson was certainly its spiritual father, and the one who first planted the principles of freedom and enlightenment in the westward movement that was to dominate the first century of our history.[54]

Jefferson had failed in 1784 to have his prohibition of slavery in the western lands adopted by the Congress. But his failure was a narrow one, which the following excerpt from a letter in 1786 indicates:

There were ten states present; six voted unanimously for it, three against it, and one was divided; and seven votes being requisite to decide the proposition affirmatively, it was lost. The voice of a single individual of the State which was divided, or of one of those which were of the negative, would have prevented this abominable crime from spreading itself over the new country. Thus we see the fate of millions unborn hanging on the tongue of one man, and heaven silent in that awful moment! But it is to be hoped that it will not always be silent, and that the friends to the rights of human nature will in the end prevail.[55]

In the Northwest Territory "the friends to the rights of human nature"—with Jefferson's powerful advocacy—did prevail. And it prevailed in another sense. What Jefferson here declares concerning the "fate of millions unborn" with respect to the ingress of slavery into virgin lands, became the iron which entered the soul of Abraham Lincoln, and formed the basis of the policy he pursued with relentless force in the years following the repeal of the Missouri Compromise in 1854.

The relationship of Jefferson to the Northwest Ordinance raises the question of the relationship of Jefferson to the Constitution in 1787. Professor Diamond thinks the Convention would have failed in its work had Jefferson been present, because of his being "too easily given to a mere libertarianism." There may, he thinks, have been a "direct intervention of Divine Providence" to keep Jefferson (and John Adams) out of Philadelphia in the fateful summer of 1787. Had these two formidable figures been present, thinks Professor Diamond, the "single clear vision of Madison would [not] have been able to prevail."[56] But there were a number of other powerful personalities present in Philadelphia who also interfered with the Madisonian vision, and one wonders why Providence didn't keep them out too. Indeed, until I read Professor Diamond's sentence, I had not known that Madison's, or anyone else's, single vision had prevailed. The Constitution was, I thought, a bundle of compromises, albeit very sensible and principled compromises—for the most part. But the compromises regarding slavery, although perhaps the outcome of necessity (as Lincoln later said), are hard to defend as principled. That cool, sober determination to force *decency* upon *democracy*, upon which Professor Diamond lavishes his finest and choicest adjectives, utterly failed when it came to the African slave trade. This trade, in which untold thousands died miserable deaths in the gruesome "middle passage" was an abomination unsurpassed in modern times until the concentration camps of Hitler and Stalin.

Madison and Jefferson enjoyed an unbroken personal and political friendship of nearly half a century. Madison, when he differed with Jefferson, had remarkable success in persuading him. Much of the radicalism which Professor Diamond imputes to Jefferson in 1787 may have arisen from the fact that he was in Paris during the incipient stages of the French Revolution, and shared in the tremendous excitement of that burgeoning event. Had he been in Philadelphia, his temper might have been different. Whether Jefferson's hot blood would have helped or hindered the cool Madison in meeting the proslavery impulse within the doors of the Convention, we certainly cannot say.

At the time of the Civil War there were nearly four million slaves. How many of them were descended from the two hundred thousand (or more) imported during the period 1787–1809 we cannot precisely say. Clearly, the number was not inconsiderable. The direct cause of the Civil War was the contest over slavery in the territories. Anything that lessened the ability or desire of the South to carry slaves into territories would have lessened the intensity of the sectional conflict. A smaller slave population would certainly have been mollifying. We repeat that we can have no idea of whether Jefferson's presence in Philadelphia would have made any eventual difference in the slave population of the United States. We do know, however, that the Northwest Ordinance, which was a Jeffersonian document, was—unlike the Constitution—uncompromising in its attempt to secure equal rights for all. We also know that it was President Jefferson who signed into law the bill outlawing as piracy the African slave trade, the first moment permitted by James Madison's constitution. But that was twenty years too late. We add as a footnote, that the only man hanged for piracy under the law Jefferson signed, was hanged during the administration of Abraham Lincoln. Lincoln refused the appeal for clemency with grim satisfaction!

Whether the Constitutional Convention's compromises with slavery were or were not prudent, might be debated endlessly. Madison defended them on the ground that there was no other way to secure the "consent" of South Carolina and Georgia to the "more perfect" Union. In the end, that "consent" was withdrawn anyway, and the Constitution that emerged from the Civil War, for at least one third of the Union, came to rest not on consent but on conquest. One wonders whether a smaller amount of conquest earlier, might have avoided a greater amount later. In any event, we venture to suggest to Professor Diamond that he take greater counsel from his cautious hero's example, in interpreting the ways of Divine Providence.

Professor Diamond's thesis, that the Declaration of Independence offered *no guidance* to the Framers of the Constitution, although uncompromisingly radical and extreme, is not unprecedented. In recent literature we find it set forth in virtually identical language, by the late Professor Willmoore Kendall. It is sufficient for present purposes to mention that Kendall denied to the equality clause of the Declaration any theoretical or practical significance for the American political tradition as a whole, or for the Constitution in particular. He insisted that the importance attributed to equality by the scholars of the tradition was post-Civil War, and derived from a fundamental "derailment" of that tradition by Abraham Lincoln. The Gettysburg Address—the primary source of that derailment— he regarded as a rhetorical trick, a trick from which virtually all the political corruptions of the twentieth century—as seen by Professor Kendall—have flowed.

Kendall, like Chief Justice Taney in the Dred Scott case, saw the mention of equality in the Declaration in relation to the Declaration's sole purpose which was "'to dissolve the political bands' which heretofore [had] connected the colonists with Great Britain." The Declaration, said Kendall, anticipated that the people thus rendered independent would shortly "engage in some sort of deliberative process to establish that form of government . . . conducive to the ends cited." But, Kendall continues, "the Declaration itself gives *no guidance* on how or in what ways such governments ought to be built." And he adds, "in *no sense* can the Declaration be considered a manual for the construction of new governments."[57]

Professor Kendall blamed Lincoln entirely for the unusual prominence given to the equality proposition of the Declaration. But before Kendall another Southerner, John C. Calhoun, had put the blame where it belonged. In a speech to the Senate, in 1848, Calhoun labelled the proposition that "all men are born free and equal" as "the most false and dangerous of all political errors."[58] In its precise form, we observe parenthetically, this proposition occurs in the Massachusetts Bill of Rights of 1780. But Calhoun correctly judged that it meant exactly the same as "all men are created equal." Calhoun also correctly judged that it was the Declaration of Independence, long before the Gettysburg Address, that gave such proposition its widest currency, and enabled it to "fix itself deeply in the public mind." Moreover, he added, contrary to what Taney would say, that "It made no necessary part of our justification in . . . declaring ourselves independent." "Nor had it," he continued "*any weight* in constructing the governments which were substituted in place of the colonial."[59] The Kendall thesis is, we see, merely the

Calhoun thesis, refurbished, and with Lincoln substituted for Jefferson as the villain of the piece. But Kendall, like Calhoun, was thoroughly devoted to the Southern ante–bellum cause. Like Calhoun, he saw the doctrine of universal and equal natural rights as thoroughly pernicious; and he saw the attack on slavery as an attack on the principles of American constitutionalism. For him as for Calhoun, the defense of slavery and the defense of constitutionalism were, in American history, inextricably intertwined. We can therefore understand perfectly why Professor Diamond—a passionate believer, he assures us, in the doctrine that all men are created equal—should find it inconvenient to mention Kendall's "no guidance" proposition as the immediate source of his own. For that immediate source is the intermediate source of the Calhoun thesis and, as such, hitherto linked to the defense of slavery. It is the apparent *severing* of this "no guidance" thesis from the defense of slavery, which constitutes Professor Diamond's uniqueness and originality.

That Professor Diamond's thesis was paradoxical we explained at the outset. It was paradoxical in maintaining that the Declaration laid upon the Framers the obligation to "secure to all people their unalienable rights," while providing *no guidance* towards that end. The paradox became something of a mystery when we observed that the Framers, giving strong guarantees to slavery in the Constitution, certainly did not secure to "all people" their unalienable rights. The same thesis as Professor Diamond's, however, appeared perfectly non-mysterious and non-paradoxical when held by the Southern defenders of slavery, who saw the Constitution itself as essentially a pro–slavery document. By presenting his thesis as being connected with an anti–slavery argument, however, Professor Diamond has compounded the paradoxicality of his paradox by some geometrical ratio. We are warned by Socrates, however, that what is paradoxical may nonetheless be true. But we are also warned by Socrates that the burden of proof is much heavier upon the one who would maintain a paradox, than upon the one who maintains what is in accordance with accepted opinion. Let us then turn to Professor Diamond's proofs.

84

When we do so, we are immediately confronted by what looks perilously like another paradox. For Professor Diamond's attempt to establish his thesis begins not with any proof, properly so called. Such a proof would be a reading of the Declaration itself, together perhaps with such collatered documents as Locke's *Second Treatise*. Instead, Professor Diamond offers us the testimony of witnesses to his thesis. And, carrying paradox still further, if that were possible, he offers as his first witness, Abraham Lincoln. The other two witnesses, we mention immediately, are Jefferson and Madison.

Now Professor Diamond's mode of argument is at least as old as that of Protagoras and Georgias. He wishes to persuade us of something that is as shocking to common sense as it is to received opinion. If however he can somehow lead us into thinking that it is not paradoxical, that it is not novel, but somehow in accordance with venerable received opinion—particularly venerable received opinion in the anti-slavery tradition—then suddenly all the burden of proof will have slipped from his shoulders to those who might contradict him.

But I would ask, who that has ever heard or read about Abraham Lincoln would think he might be a witness to such a thesis? Who would think that Lincoln could be made to testify to the doctrine of John C. Calhoun? Who would believe that Abraham Lincoln thought that the Declaration of Independence offered no guidance to the Framers—and hence to the interpreters—of the Constitution? What Boy Scout who has recited the Gettysburg Address, either at Lincoln's birthplace, or at the Lincoln Memorial in Washington, ever suspected that the beginning and the end of that immortal oration were unrelated to each other? Who ever doubted that dedication to the proposition that all men are created equal meant simultaneously dedication to framing a government, of, by, and for the people? Is not the principle of equality, and the principle of popular government—or democracy—one and the same, according to Lincoln? "As I would not be a *slave*, so I would not be a *master*. This expresses my idea of democracy. Whatever differs from this, to the extent of the difference, is no democracy."[60]

We have referred more than once to Lincoln's rebuttal of Taney and Douglas on the Dred Scott decision, in which he speaks of the

Declaration kicking off the King and Lords of Great Britain. How can that, and innumerable other similar passages in Lincoln's writings and speeches be interpreted away to make Lincoln a witness to the thesis that the Declaration is, in Professor Diamond's words, "neutral on the question of forms of government." It is one thing to dispute the correctness of Lincoln's view of the Declaration, but it is quite another to say what it *is*.

How does Professor Diamond propose to overturn more than a century of received opinion concerning Lincoln? All his evidence is drawn from the inferences he makes from two brief quotations from Lincoln's remarks in Independence Hall, in February, 1861, remarks from which we have already quoted. We reproduce these quotations, as they occur in Professor Diamond's text, in their entirety. We do so, moreover, with the single sentence which links the two in Professor Diamond's text, and with the entire commentary in which Professor Diamond sets forth for us this radically new interpretation of Lincoln.

> All the political *sentiments* I entertain have been drawn *so far I have been able to draw them*, from the *sentiments* which originated, and were given to the world from this hall in which we stand. I have never had a *feeling* politically that did not spring from the *sentiments* embodied in the Declaration of Independence [All emphasis supplied by Professor Diamond].

"Now this sentiment [writes Professor Diamond] that Lincoln drew from the Declaration was that document's passionate devotion to the principle of liberty."

> . . . something in that Declaration giving liberty, not alone to the people of this country, but hope to the world for all future time. It was that which gave promise that in due time the weights should be lifted from the shoulders of all men, and that all should have an equal chance. This is the sentiment embodied in that Declaration of Independence.

"We must take careful heed of Lincoln's remarkable stress, throughout this speech from which we are quoting [continues Professor Diamond], on the words feeling and sentiment. He carefully limits his indebtedness to the Declaration only to certain sentiments and feelings, that is, to the spirit of liberty within which he conceives American government and its institutions. Indeed, he could not have done otherwise, for there is nothing in the Declaration which

86

goes beyond that sentiment of liberty. As we shall see, noble document that the Declaration is, indispensable source of the feelings
and sentiments of Americans and of the spirit of liberty in which
their institutions were conceived, the Declaration is devoid of
guidance as to what those institutions should be."[61]

What has Professor Diamond discovered in Lincoln's words, to
justify this staggering novelty in interpretation? The answer is,
quite literally, *nothing*. In passages in which Lincoln appears to be
saying that he owes *everything* politically dear to him to the Declaration, Professor Diamond would have us believe that Lincoln is
saying, or implying, that the Declaration is "devoid of guidance."
Now this is mere hypercritical criticism; it is interpretation in a
void. Professor Kristol cheerfully tells us not to take too seriously,
or to ignore, whatever he finds in his sources that he does not like.
But Professor Diamond, when he does not find what he wants,
insists nonetheless upon putting it there. He weaves an interpretation around a text like those fabulous weavers who made the
Emperor's new clothes.

Professor Diamond's interpretation depends wholly upon the
peculiar negative inference he draws from Lincoln's choice of the
words "sentiment" and "feeling." He coordinates these, in his own
mind and, he hopes, in ours, with something he calls "the spirit of
liberty." This spirit of liberty is a kind of disembodied affection,
within which our "institutions were conceived," but which conception in itself is "devoid of guidance as to what those institutions
should be." Professor Diamond knows that Lincoln at Gettysburg
spoke of the new nation being "conceived in liberty." But Professor
Diamond should have reflected that there is no conception in
nature—nor even in the supernatural conception of traditional
Christianity—in which the *form* of the thing conceived is not
implanted at the moment of conception. The idea of a conception
neutral with respect to the form of the thing conceived would be a
monster. Certainly in the Gettysburg Address the relationship
implied between conception and birth is one of traditional, biologi-
cal teleology. Similarly, the idea of the birth and re-birth of freedom
draws upon the idea of the birth and re-birth of the soul, in traditional
Christianity. In Lincoln's precise analogy, the release of the nation

from the sin of slavery corresponds to the release of the world from original sin. The Civil War becomes then a kind of crucifixion and resurrection of the nation, corresponding to that of the Christ in theological doctrine.

But what of Lincoln's use of the words "sentiment" and "feeling?" Do they not in some measure or manner imply *some* limitation upon what Lincoln thought he owed to the Declaration, as distinct from the Constitution? The most that one can state affirmatively, is that these words might have contained some negative implications, if used by Professor Diamond in an undergraduate political science lecture. But as used by Abraham Lincoln, as President-elect, on the eve of his inauguration, and on the eve of the Civil War, they did not and could not. That they did not, I propose to show by reference to Lincoln's customary use of these words in other contexts. That they could not, I propose to show as a matter of political necessity. Any denial of the guiding role of the Declaration in the interpretation of the Constitution, such as Professor Diamond attributes to Lincoln, would have been destructive of everything he stood for at that critical moment.

First, as to Lincoln's usage.

> August 21, 1858. In this and like communities, public sentiment is everything. With public sentiment nothing can fail; without it, nothing can succeed. Consequently he who molds public sentiment goes deeper than he who enacts statutes or pronounces decisions.[62]
>
> December 10, 1856. Our government rests in public opinion. Whoever can change public opinion, can change the government practically so much.[63]
>
> September 17, 1859. In the first place, we know that in a government like this, in a government of the people, where the voice of all the men of the country substantially enters into the execution,—or administration rather of the government, what lies at the bottom of all of it, is public opinion.[64]

And finally:

> March 28, 1864. . . . the great loyal public sentiment of the country, which is, indeed, the foundation of all else that is valuable in this great national trial.[65]

We take it then as proved, that "public sentiment" and "public opinion" are synonymous and interchangeable in Lincoln's usage, and any advantages that Professor Diamond might seek to gain for his interpretation, stemming from the choice of the expression "sentiments" as opposed to "opinions" is without foundation.

But what of the word "feeling," upon which Professor Diamond also lays much stress. Again, we give examples of Lincoln's usage of this word in another context. We quote at some length a famous passage in the Peoria speech (the longest Lincoln ever made) of October 16, 1854. This speech was given many times, and virtually all his speeches of the later 1850s were developed from it.

> What next?—Free them [the slaves], and make them politically and socially our equals? My own feelings will not admit of this; and if mine would, we well know that those of the great mass of white people will not. Whether this feeling accords with justice and sound judgment, is not the sole question, if indeed, it is any part of it. A universal feeling, whether well or ill founded, can not be safely disregarded.[66]

Is it not clear that, used in a political context, "feeling" like "sentiment" becomes a virtual synonym for "opinion." Obviously, the universal feelings, to which Lincoln refers in the last sentence quoted, becomes known and manifest to politicians like Lincoln by responses in their audiences, which are interpreted to be their *opinions*.

But Lincoln also believed in a kind of moral sense, which gave a particular meaning and propriety to his use of words such as sentiment and feeling. Consider the following, also from the Peoria speech.

> The great majority, south as well as north, have human sympathies, of which they can no more divest themselves than they can their sensibility to physical pain. These sympathies in the bosoms of the southern people, manifest in many ways, their sense of the wrong of slavery. . . .[67]

We see the *sense* of the wrong of slavery becomes, by analogy, virtually a *sensation* of that wrong. That sensation can quite properly become a *feeling* or *sentiment* which thereupon becomes the foundation of public *opinion*.

We turn now to the political considerations governing Lincoln's choice of words, on the eve of his inauguration. In the first of the quotations selected by Professor Diamond, Lincoln says

> All the political *sentiments* I entertain have been drawn, *so far as I have been*

able to draw them . . . from the sentiments embodied in the Declaration of Independence.

Professor Diamond has italicized for emphasis, not only "sentiments," but "so far as I have been able to draw them". He would have us believe that Lincoln could not draw *all* his political sentiments (or opinions) from the Declaration, because the Declaration is "devoid of guidance" on many of the political topics upon which Lincoln evidently possessed opinions or sentiments. But again, Professor Diamond is being grossly and needlessly hypercritical. "So far as I have been able" means no more, in this context, than "to the best of my ability." Any limitation here referred to, is a limitation *upon Lincoln*, not upon the Declaration. It is merely an expression of Lincoln's modesty. To express an opinion of the limitation *of the Declaration*, in this time or place, would have been utterly unbecoming and self-defeating. Lincoln's entire policy, culminating in his election, was a policy which depended upon finding the meaning of the Constitution *in* the Declaration of Independence. Anything that, by the remotest inference, weakened the force of the Declaration, as a guide to the meaning of the Constitution, would have weakened Lincoln's hold upon public opinion, as he approached the crisis of secession and war. As Lincoln spoke those words in Independence Hall, he had already completed the basic text of his inaugural address. That address included the following passage.

> All profess to be content in the Union, if all constitutional rights can be maintained. Is it true then that any right, plainly written in the Constitution, has been denied? I think not . . . no organic law can ever be framed with a provision specifically applicable to every question which may occur. . . . Shall fugitives from labor be surrendered by national or by State authority? The Constitution does not expressly say. *May* Congress prohibit slavery in the territories? The Constitution does not expressly say. *Must* Congress protect slavery in the territories? The Constitution does not expressly say.
>
> From questions of this class spring all our constitutional controversies, and we divide upon them into majorities and minorities.[68]

On the matter of the rendition of fugitive slaves, Lincoln was a "conservative" within the ranks of the Republican Party, strongly insisting that this was one of those unpleasant obligations "nominated in the bond" of the Constitution from which there was no just escape. But the two other questions went to the heart of the sectional controversy. The Republicans insisted that Congress *did* have the power to prohibit slavery in the territories, and that it should exercise that power. But Chief Justice Taney, in his opinion in the case of Dred Scott, had said that Congress had no such power. The only power Congress had, Taney declared, was the power, coupled with the duty, of protecting the slave owner in his rights. This was interpreted politically in the South to mean that Congress had a *duty* to protect slavery in the territories. The Southern position, in 1860, thus came to rest upon two parts of the Constitution. The one was the so–called fugitive slave clause, Article IV, Section 3, paragraph 3. The other was that clause of the Fifth Amendment which declared that "No person shall be . . . deprived of life, liberty, or property, without due process of law . . ." If a Negro was a human person within the meaning of the Constitution, then the Fifth Amendment laid an injunction upon the United States, that he not be deprived of his liberty when he came under the jurisdiction of the United States, in the territories of the United States. This, of course, was Lincoln's position, and that of the Republican Party. But if the Negro's character as a chattel must take precedence of his character as a human person, then his owner might not be deprived of him, when he migrated with him into that same territory. This was the position of those Southern Democrats, who bolted the Charleston Democratic Convention. What is crucial to the matter is this: The Constitution was perfectly ambiguous with respect to whether it commanded freedom or slavery in the territories. It could be said, with equal reason, to treat Negro slaves as chattels (by virtue of the fugitive slave clause), and as human persons (by virtue of the phrase "three fifths of all other Persons" in Article I.) Because of this, Chief Justice Taney himself turned to the Declaration for the fundamental premise of his opinion. He insisted that the proposition of human equality there did *not* include Negroes (whether slave or free). Constitutionally, he maintained, Negroes were not and could not become citizens of the United States, but must be regarded as "beings of an inferior order [with] no rights which the white man was bound to respect."[69] It was then quite literally the case, in 1861, that the interpretation of the Declaration, and its application to "all our constitutional controversies" was at the bottom of the entire North–South dispute. Taken by itself, the Constitution of the United States, for all the coolness, moderation, and sobriety, for which Professor Diamond so justly praises it, was, at that moment, a mere blind thing. Like the nation which as a whole no longer accepted it, it was divided against itself. It could yield no coherent meaning of its own. It became again a living, vital, organic thing, only as Lincoln applied the touchstone of the Declaration to it. Happily, it is too late for Professor Diamond's discovery that it supplied Lincoln with "no guidance" to have consequences as pernicious as they are absurd.

After certifying Abraham Lincoln as holding the thesis of John C. Calhoun, Professor Diamond turns to the no less difficult task of adding the names of Madison and Jefferson to his list of witnesses.

> In addition to inferring this [viz., "no guidance" from the Declaration] from Lincoln's speech, we have also the highest possible authority for this conclusion: namely, the testimony of the "Father of the Constitution," James Madison, and the acceptance of that testimony by the author of the Declaration, Thomas Jefferson.[70]

Madison and Jefferson are in some ways even harder for Professor Diamond to turn to his purpose. Although he disregarded the manifest tenor of all of Lincoln's speeches and writings—up to and including the Gettysburg Address—Professor Diamond at least quoted a substantial and unbowdlerized portion of *one* speech. It is true that his interpretation proved, on inspection, to be a mere interpolation of his own opinion. In the present case, however, we get nothing but a few chopped and cut phrases taken out of context from a private letter by Madison to Jefferson. (There is one complete sentence.) But genuine understanding of such a letter is governed by many unstated political facts, and its nuances reflect a complex private relationship. Professor Diamond invents a simple and foreshortened context, from which he happily derives *dicta* which he imputes to Madison and Jefferson. But these are no more to be found in anything actually said by these men, than was the *dictum* imputed to Lincoln, that the Declaration of Independence was "devoid of guidance" with respect to the form or meaning of the

Constitution. Moreover, we will find something here even more extraordinary than Professor Diamond's exotic interpretations. We will find Madison and Jefferson agreeing, and *saying explicity*, that the Declaration of Independence, so far from supplying *no guidance*, is in fact *first* among those documents said to be the *"best guides,"* to the principles of the government of the State of Virginia and of the United States. How Professor Diamond reconciles his suppression of these passages with his scholarly conscience, we leave it to him to explain.[71]

We feel obliged now to quote the full text of that portion of Professor Diamond's Distinguished Lecture, in which he allegedly construes the testimony of Madison and Jefferson. We must also, in the sequel, quote at some length the documentary evidence relating to Madison's and Jefferson's actual opinions of the matters under consideration. However tedious this procedure is, we believe it indispensable when questions of selective quotation, misconstrued context, and of suppressed evidence, are at stake.

> In 1825 the two patriarchs of the American founding engaged in a correspondence regarding a possible required reading list for students at the Law School of the University of Virginia. They took it for granted, as Madison said, that the students should be required to read books that would inculcate "the true doctrines of liberty" which are "exemplified in our political system." But it is not easy, Madison wrote, to find books that will be both "guides and guards" for the purpose. The work of John Locke, for example, Madison went on, was "admirably calculated to impress on young minds the right of nations to establish their own governments and to inspire a love of free ones." (This "love" would seem to be exactly what Lincoln meant by the "sentiment" of the Declaration.) But Locke could not teach those future lawyers how to protect "our Republican charters," that is, how to protect the American federal and state constitutions from being corrupted by false interpretations, because Locke gave insufficient guidance regarding the nature of our republican institutions.
>
> Now to put these words in a letter to Jefferson, who, as the author of the Declaration, had clearly drawn inspiration from John Locke, would seem to be cutting pretty close to the bone. But Madison had no reason to hesitate in thus writing to his old friend because he could count on Jefferson's calmly agreeing with his view. Indeed, he proceeded to make his point even more explicitly. "The Declaration of Independence," Madison continued, "though rich in fundamental principles, and saying everything that could be said in the same number of words"—it never hurts to be gentle with an author's pride no matter how close a friend he is—"falls nearly under a like observa-

tion." What his careful eighteenth century language is saying is plainly this: The principles of Locke and of Jefferson's Declaration are infinitely valuable for inspiring in young minds a proper love of free government; but that is all that those principles reach to. The Declaration, Madison is saying and Jefferson cheerfully agrees, offers no guidance for the construction of free government and hence offers no aid in protecting the American form of government under the Constitution. For that purpose, Madison does not scruple to add, one must turn to *The Federalist* "as the most authentic exposition of the text of the federal Constitution." In short, the patriarchs Jefferson and Madison agree with Lincoln, as I have interpreted him, in their understanding of the noble but limited work of the Declaration.[72]

This is the complete exposition by Professor Diamond, as evidence of Jefferson's and Madison's support for the proposition that the Declaration offers "no guidance" and "no aid" either for the construction or the interpretation of the Constitution.

Professor Diamond has drawn all his brief quotations and references from a letter of Madison to Jefferson, dated February 8, 1825. This letter is clearly in response to a communication from Jefferson to Madison, since Madison begins his letter thus. "I have looked with attention over your intended proposal of a text-book for the Law School."[73] Now I have not identified with certainty Jefferson's letter to Madison. But we are told by Jefferson's biographers that he wrote substantially the same thing to Joseph Cabell, at the same time.[74] What appears to be the relevant letter reads, in part, as follows:

> In most public seminaries textbooks are prescribed to each of the several schools, as *norma docendi* in that school; and this is generally done by authority of the trustees. I should not propose this generally in our University, because I believe none of us are so much at the heights of science . . . as to undertake this, and therefore it will be better left to the professors until occasion of interference shall be given. But there is one branch in which we are the best judges, in which heresies may be taught, of so interesting a character to our own State and to the United States, as to make it a duty in us to lay down the principles to be taught. It is that of government. Mr. Gilmer being withdrawn, we know not who his successor may be. He may be a Richmond lawyer, or one of that school of quondam federalism, now consolidation. It is our duty to guard against the principles being disseminated among our youth, and the diffusion of that poison, by a previous prescription of the texts to be followed in their discourses.[75]

Now we see from the foregoing that although Professor Diamond's characterization of this correspondence as one concerning "a possible required reading list for students" may be correct as far as it goes, it does not go far enough. Madison represents Jefferson as seeking, not a reading list—or even a required reading list—but a textbook. This is not exactly the same thing. From Jefferson's letter we learn that his primary concern is not the reading of the *students* but the *norma docendi*—the instructional principles—which the *teachers* are *to be bound to follow* "in their discourses." And the burden of Madison's letter is to point out to Jefferson, tactfully but firmly, that there is no book, nor are there any books, which will perform the function of *norma docendi* in the sense Jefferson desired. This, to repeat, is to guard against the poison of "quondam federalism, now consolidation," being dissseminated among our youth. When Madison, as quoted by Professor Diamond, says that it is not easy to find "guards and guides" to inculcate "the true doctrines of liberty" exemplified "in our political system," *this* is what he refers to; although one would never be able to guess it from Professor Diamond's text. Yet it is in reference to *this*—namely, guarding against the poison of "quondam federalism, now consolidation"— that Madison discusses the adequacy of different books and documents. Jefferson, we discover, had already suggested Sidney, Locke, the Declaration of Independence, and Madison's Virginia Report of 1799–1800, as forming the body of the "text-book." Madison agrees with these suggestions, but he points out the limitations of each item in turn. Then he himself suggests adding Washington's Inaugural and Farewell Address, for reasons to which we will return. He also suggests that Jefferson "relax the absoluteness of [the] injunction" in his draft, meaning thereby that he wished to see a little loosening of the instructional straitjacket Jefferson wished to impose.

What then was this poison called "quondam federalism, now consolidation," against whose dissemination among the youth, Jefferson was so anxious to guard? It meant, in the main, the liberal interpretation of the Constitution by finding a great many "implied powers" in the "necessary and proper" clause of Article I, Section 9, of the Constitution, as well as by finding an independent grant of power in the "general welfare" clause of the same section. The poison of consolidation had first entered the body politic under the Consti-

95

tution by the chartering of the first Bank of the United States in 1791. The clearest and most concise expressions of the differences between liberal and strict construction are, to this day, the opposing opinions of Hamilton and Jefferson on the constitutionality of the bank. In Jefferson's political theology, liberal construction meant consolidation—that is, the transfer of powers Jefferson though belonged to the states, from the states to the central government. Jefferson believed that powers exercised from the center were necessarily less under the observation, and hence less under the vigilant control, of the people. Such transfer of powers from the states, he called toryism, and monarchism. That was the issue which led him to call the election of 1800 a revolution as great as (or greater than) that of 1776. The flaming manifesto of his faith in this period was his draft of the Kentucky Resolutions of 1798.

One might have thought that Jefferson's subsequent experience, in the purchase of Louisiana, and Madison's, in signing into law the bill chartering the second Bank of the United States, would have tempered this creed. In Madison's case, it undoubtedly did. But in his last years the creed of 1800 flamed in Jefferson with all its old fervor, a fervor certainly fed in 1825 by his distrust of President John Quincy Adams, and his consuming hatred of Chief Justice John Marshall, both of them disciples, in the crucial respects, of his old foe, Alexander Hamilton. It is one of the ironies of Jefferson's career that, having won all the political battles that he could, he died with two such supposed foes of his principles in power in Washington!

In 1821 Jefferson had been persuaded to endorse John Taylor's turgid and tiresome book, *Construction Construed*. Although it took ten times as long to say what Jefferson himself had said far better, both in the bank opinion of 1791, and the Kentucky Resolutions of 1798, it also contained some suitable polemics against the opinions of Chief Justice John Marshall. And so Jefferson wrote that

> on all important questions it contains the *true political faith, to which every catholic republican should steadfastly hold.* It should be put in the hands of all our functionaries, authoritatively as a standing instruction and true exposition of our Constitution, as understood at the time we agreed to it [Emphasis added].[76]

Now Thomas Jefferson did not become the Father of the University of Virginia, merely because of an abstract commitment to the glories of science and of higher education. He was enraged at the sums of money that wealthy Virginia families spent every year to send their sons away to such schools as Harvard and Yale, and he wanted that money spent in Virginia instead. But worse than the money that they took *out* of the state, were the ideas of New England federalism that they brought *into* it. The Law School of the University of Virginia (Jefferson had to modify his original plan to have chairs of both law *and* government) was to be the center from which a counter-offensive, both in Virginia and the nation, was to be launched, by a fundamentalist Virginia republicanism, against "quondam federal-ism, now consolidation." In a later letter to Madison Jefferson expressed this thought as follows:

> nearly all the young brood of lawyers . . . suppose themselves indeed to be whigs because they no longer know what whiggism or republicanism means. It is in our seminary that that vestal flame is to be kept alive; it is thence it is to spread anew over our own and the sister States. If we are true and vigilant in our trust, within a dozen or twenty years a majority of our own Legislature will be from one school, and many disciples will have carried its doctrines home with them to their several States, and will have leavened thus the whole mass.[77]

Without understanding—as Madison thoroughly did—Jefferson's passionate concern to make the University of Virginia an evangelical center for the counter-reformation of whiggism or republicanism, such sparse quotations from Madison's letter as Professor Diamond gives are utterly unintelligible. Yet Madison himself was not in thorough sympathy with this concern. In 1825, the issue of strict versus liberal construction turned mainly on the matter of internal improvements. In December 1825, Jefferson prepared a thundering new set of Virginia Resolutions—which he did not, in the end, press upon the legislature—in which the unconstitutionality of internal improvements was denounced. But on February 17, 1825—just nine days after the letter about the text-book or reading list for the Law School—Madison wrote to Jefferson on this topic, as follows:

> Were the unauthorized schemes of internal improvement as disagreeable to a majority of the people and of the States as they are deemed advantageous, who can doubt the different reasonings and result that would be observed within the walls of Congress? The will of the nation being omnipotent for

97

right, is so for wrong also; and the will of the nation being in the majority, the minority must submit to that danger of oppression as an evil infinitely less than the danger to the whole nation from a will independent of it. I consider the question as to canals, etc., as decided, therefore, because sanctioned by the nation under the permanent influence of benefit to the major part of it. . . .[78]

This letter is of incalculable import to anyone studying the political thought of James Madison, and we cannot begin to indicate its full scope. For our immediate purpose, we note the following. First, Madison concedes that, under the stimulus of utility, a national majority may override the bounds of the Constitution. This of course is what the multi–factioned extended republic for which Madison contended in *The Federalist* was designed to prevent, but which Madison had conceded in number fifty–one, would sometimes nonetheless occur. Here Madison anticipates the premise upon which Calhoun was to build in the *Exposition and Protest* of 1828. But whereas Calhoun was to insist that the existence of a majority faction demanded an "auxiliary device" to counter it—such as nullification—Madison merely and rather lamely says that we may as well submit to it as a lesser evil. Now Madison would never have arrived at this conclusion, had he shared Jefferson's fears of "consolidation" arising from internal improvements. Jefferson, and other Virginia fundamentalists, were viewing internal improvements with all the horror with which Jefferson and Madison had once viewed the Alien and Sedition Acts. And Madison did not share their apprehension.

But Madison's argument, in favor of submitting to the decision of the national majority, even if it had acted unconstitutionally, is not unprecedented. At bottom, it is the same argument to which Jefferson himself had submitted in acceding to his friends' advice concerning the purchase of Louisiana. Jefferson believed that the enabling legislation for implementing that historic act was unauthorized by the Constitution, and required an amendment to the Constitution. But the approval of the majority, under the stimulus of the utility felt from the purchase, was substituted for strict constitutionalism. Madison may also have been conveying to Jefferson a tacit reminder of that precedent. It is possible also that the storm of nullification, which was to burst not long after Jefferson's death, was already visible, as a cloud no bigger than a man's hand, to Madison.

And so he was also doing his gentle but shrewd best to keep Jefferson from giving his authority—any more than it had already been given—to doctrines of states rights which might, in the future, be far more pernicious than the "quondam federalism" of the past.

We return now to Madison's letter to Jefferson of February 8, 1825, better able to catch the drift or tenor of its argument. We recall that Madison began by saying that he had looked "with attention" at Jefferson's proposal of a text-book. This, we may now gather, implied less than full approval of the project. He continues:

> It is certainly very material that the true doctrines of liberty, as exemplified in our Political System, should be inculcated on those who are to sustain and may administer it. It is, at the same time, not easy to find standard books that will be both guides and guards for the purpose. Sidney & Locke are admirably calculated to impress on young minds the right of Nations to establish their own Governments, and to inspire a love of free ones, but afford no aid in guarding our Republican Charters against constructive violations. The Declaration of Independence, though rich in fundamental principles and saying every thing that could be said in the same number of words, falls nearly under a like observation.[79]

Madison says that neither Locke nor Sidney nor the Declaration "afford . . . aid in guarding our Republican charters against *constructive* violations." Of course they could not. The writings referred to were all produced before "our Republican Charters," meaning before our national or state constitutions existed. More specifically, they were written before the elaborate system of American federalism, a system "partly national, partly federal," had been invented or, so far as we know, even conceived in the mind of man. Professor Diamond himself has written well concerning the absolute novelty of the "federalism" that emerged from the Convention of 1787.[80] On the question of the proper distribution of powers between the central government and the state governments, and the proper mode of constitutional interpretation to preserve that proper distribution, it would of course have been impossible to find any "guide" or "guard" written before 1787. The most that Jefferson could have expected of the Declaration, is that it would alert mankind to the question of whether any particular political system did or did not act to secure their unalienable rights. But he would never have thought that it could provide guidance to how the particular theories of how

99

to operate the federal system of 1787 would act or react upon this question. Professor Diamond's suggestion that Madison was being particularly tender with Jefferson's pride here, is wholly gratuitous. But what about *The Federalist*? Professor Diamond would have us think that Madison says that "one must turn to *The Federalist*" to find exactly that "guidance for the construction of free government and . . . aid in protecting the American form of free government under the Constitution" which was not to be found in the Declaration. Here is what Madison does say.

> The "Federalist" may fairly enough be regarded as the most authentic exposition of the text of the Federal Constitution, as understood by the body which prepared and the authority which accepted it. Yet it did not foresee all the misconstructions which have occurred, nor prevent some that it did foresee. And what equally deserves remark, neither of the great rival parties have acquiesced in all its comments.[81]

We may summarize the foregoing by saying that Madison confesses that *The Federalist*, as a means of counteracting the poison of consolidation is nearly, if not perfectly useless. That it may provide guidance for the construction of free government may be true; but that as we shall see is also true of the Declaration. The guidance that each supplies could also be said to supplement the other. But as far as providing that guard against misconstruction desired by Jefferson, *The Federalist* has *no* value. It is my opinion—and one I believe that is supported by Professor Diamond's other writings—that *The Federalist* leans far more towards liberal or loose construction than otherwise. Its most powerful argument is that the rights of all are far more apt to be secured in a large or extended republic than in smaller ones. In our federal system, that means that the multiplicity of factions in the arena of national politics is a better guardian of the rights of the minor party—that is, that it is a better guardian against the tyranny of the majority—than is possible in the smaller republics of the states. But if this is the case, then the transfer of otherwise reserved powers, from the states to the central government, would not necessarily represent a diminution of liberty. It might, in fact, represent its enlargement. I would go farther even, and suggest that, if all the truth were known, it might be found that the poison of consolidation, if it entered American politics anywhere, did so with

The Federalist.[82] Madison's remarks to Jefferson, about *The Feder-alist* are then uneasy and apologetic. They are anything but the confident assertions imagined by Professor Diamond.

Madison's final remarks about *The Federalist* are less significant but are amusing indications of his recognition of its relative unim-portance in Jefferson's scheme.

> It may, nevertheless, be admissible as a School book, if any will be that goes so much into detail. It has been actually admitted into two Universities, if not more—those of Harvard and Rhode Island; but probably at the choice of the Professor, without any injunction from the superior authority.[83]

Then Madison turns to the "Virginia Document of 1799." This was the Report that Madison prepared for a Committee of the House of Delegates in December, 1799. It was a defense of the Virginia Resolutions of 1798, against the objections brought forward in the different state legislatures in the previous year. It was the most elaborate and reasoned exposition of the Republican opposition to the Alien and Sedition Acts. It did not have the flaming rhetoric of Jefferson's draft of the Kentucky Resolutions, but its moderation of tone, and its close and comprehensive reasoning, made it just that foundation stone for a constitutional states rights position that *The Federalist* was not. Professor Diamond makes no mention of it at all.

> With respect to the Virginia Document of 1799, there may be more room for hesitation. Though corresponding with the predominant sense of the nation, being of local origin, and having reference to a state of parties not yet extinct, an absolute prescription of it might excite prejudices against the University as under party banners, and induce the more bigoted to withhold from it their sons, even when destined for other than the studies of the Law School. It may be added, that the Document is not on every point satisfactory to all who belong to the same party. Are we sure that to our brethren of the Board it is so?[84]

The "Virginia Document of 1799" is the only one of those proposed by Jefferson which in any way addresses itself to the issue of coun-teracting the "poison" of "consolidation." If Jefferson had been able to do what he wanted, he would almost certainly have preferred the Kentucky Resolutions, or a book like *Construction Construed*, which he had already denominated as containing "the true political faith, to which every catholic republican should steadfastly hold." But

Jefferson knew—although not sufficiently well, according to Madison—that one man's catholicism is another's heretical sectarianism. The more satisfactory a book was to him, the less so it would be to others. The Virginia Report was, in fact, the most temperate and most conciliatory of all the great documents produced by the bitter party controversy of the 1790s. And yet even it, warns Madison, is likely to give the University too local, and too partisan, an identification. But Madison knew and undoubtedly shared Jefferson's hope that the University of Virginia would become national in its influence. "An absolute prescription of it" might unnecessarily excite prejudices against the University, and even give rise to internal division. It is, to repeat, that "absolute prescription" which Jefferson wishes to enforce, that lay at the heart of the difficulty. Madison is trying to tell Jefferson that the truth is going to have to rely upon its own inherent powers, without the support of authority to enforce it! He cagily and shrewdly frames this thought in these sentences, which certainly should rank among the profoundest ever written by an American statesman.

> In framing a political creed, a like difficulty occurs as in the case of religion, though the public right be very different in the two cases. If the articles be in very general terms, they do not answer the purpose; if in very particular terms, they divide and exclude where meant to unite and fortify. The best that can be done in our case seems to be to avoid the two extremes, by referring to selected standards, without requiring an unqualified conformity to them, which, indeed, might not in every instance be possible.[85]

The objection to Locke, Sidney, and the Declaration, is that, being in "very general terms" they do not answer Jefferson's purpose, which is to counteract the poison of consolidation. It is not that these works provide "no guidance." They do provide guidance to all partisans of free, republican regimes. They provide the same kind of guidance as would be sought by anyone seeking to establish a church upon the foundation of, let us say, the New Testament, as distinct from either the Old Testament alone, or the Koran, or as distinct from any non-Biblical religion. That is to say, a book might direct people to Christianity, and away from any other religion, without attempting to decide for them the issues which divide Protestants and Catholics, or which divide any of the innumerable sects which ostensibly share a common allegiance to the Gospels.

Madison's recommendation then is for books which are not too general to be useless, nor too partisan to be divisive. But he also recommends against requiring too "unqualified conformity." Then he shrewdly suggests adding to Jefferson's list, "the Inaugural Speech and the Farewell Address of President Washington." These, he says, "contain nothing which is not good; unless it be the laudatory reference in the Address to the Treaty of 1795 with Great Britain, which ought not to weigh against the sound sentiments characterizing it."[86] The foregoing is, however prefaced with a more substantial reason, viz., "They may help down what might be less readily swallowed." We observe that the list had contained three items dealing with American government: the Declaration, *The Federalist*, The Virginia Document of 1799. The two additional items would bring the number to five, leaving the Virginia Document in the center. This was certainly the one which needed help in being swallowed, as it was certainly the only one that could be imagined as counteracting the "poison" of "quondam federalism, now consolidation."

But Madison's recommendation concerning the *norma docendi* of government at the University of Virginia, did not stop there. His last word is one which agrees with what Socrates said in the *Phaedrus*, and Plato *in propria persona* in the *Seventh Letter*, concerning the differences between writings, on the one hand, and living speech, on the other.

> After all, the most effectual safeguard against heretical intrusions into the school of politics will be an able and orthodox Professor, whose course of instruction will be an example to his successors, and may carry with it a sanction from the Visitors.[87]

Jefferson wanted to control the "course of instruction" *a priori*. But Madison, despite his speaking of heresy and orthodoxy with Jefferson as if they were a couple of bishops, warns that this is impossible. He may have wished tacitly to remind Jefferson that the two most successful "professors" of all, Socrates and Jesus, gave only oral instruction—oral instruction which, however, founded literary traditions. But we must bear in mind that Madison's objections to the Declaration form part of a comprehensive set of objections to *all* authoritative texts. There is no basis whatsover for Professor Diamond's singling out the Declaration as providing less guidance than any other. In fact, as we shall now see, among the books furnishing imperfect guidance, the Declaration is given the post of Honor. For Madison ends his letter with a "Sketch," which begins thus:

> And on the distinctive principles of the Government of our own State, and of that of the United States, the best guides are to be found in:
>
> 1. The Declaration of Independence, as the fundamental act of Union of these States.
> 2. The book known by the title of the "Federalist. . . ."
> 3. The Resolutions of the General Assembly of Virginia in 1799. . . .
> 4. The Inaugural Speech and Farewell Address of President Washington. . . .[88]

Jefferson, alas, in his Resolutions for the Board of Visitors of the University of Virginia, seems not to have listened too attentively to Madison's advice against requiring an "unqualified conformity." The Resolutions require that *no* principles of government "shall be inculcated which are incompatible with those on which the Constitutions of this State and of the United States were genuinely based, in the common opinion."

Jefferson's list begins by recommending Locke and Sidney, as before, "for the general principles of liberty and the rights of man, in nature and society." When he comes to the "distinctive principles of the government of our State, and of that of the United States," Jefferson follows the enumeration of Madison, with the single exception that he drops from number four the "Inaugural Speech" of Washington. But neither Madison nor Jefferson seems to have hesitated for a moment in affirming that among those works which may be called "the *best guides*" to the "distinctive principles of government of our State and of that of the United States," the *first* was the Declaration of Independence.[89]

Having completed the cross-examination of Professor Diamond's witnesses—so to speak—we turn to the direct examination of Professor Diamond. More precisely, we examine his attempt to sustain his interpretation of the Declaration by his own "independent reading of the text of the Declaration." Once again, we are obliged to tax our readers' patience by extended quotation of those passages in Professor Diamond's Distinguished Lecture which convey this "independent reading." If some of those passages add little or nothing to the interpretation, our readers may at least see for themselves that we have omitted nothing material. "The relevant passage," Professor Diamond begins,

> is the one usually printed as the second paragraph, the passage dealing with the truths the Declaration holds to be self-evident. Now this does not, by the way, mean evident to everyone, as it has come to be thought in these disbelieving days. The mockers say—Those truths aren't evident to me; I'm into a different bag, and since they aren't evident to me they cannot truly be truths. The author of the Declaration knew that these truths would not be self-evident to kings and nobles, not to predetermined adversaries, not to anyone of insufficient or defective vision. Indeed Jefferson knew that those truths had not hitherto been held as evident by the vast majority of mankind. But, by self-evidence, the Declaration does not refer to the selves to whom the truths are evident, but rather means that the evidentness of the truths is contained within the truths themselves. That is, these truths are not to be reached at the end of a chain reasoning: they are not the fruit of supporting evidence, inference, and argument; but rather, carrying the evidence of their truthfulness within themselves, their truth is to be grasped by a kind of direct seeing or perception. And, we may add, their truthfulness was to be vindicated by the excellence of their consequences. It would be by means of triumphant freedom that others would be able to see and then to hold those truths to be self-evident. It was up to the American Revolution and the future American regime to vindicate them.[90]

Up to this point Professor Diamond's interpretation—or explanation—of the Declaration is a strange mixture of truth and error. He is certainly correct in his assertion and reassertion that self-evident truths have their truthfulness in themselves, and do not depend for that truthfulness upon whether anyone perceives them to be true. When he says that such truths are not to be reached at the end of a chain of reasoning, he is also correct. Self-evident propositions are axiomatic, and are not inferred or deduced from antecedent propositions. But when he says that they are not the fruit of supporting *evidence*, as distinct from antecedent *propositions*, he is clearly wrong. To be self-evident means, as it says, to have evidence, and to have evidence which supports. The evidence which supports axiomatic premises in empirical matters—and an assertion about all human beings is an empirical judgment of the mind—is *inductive*, and the judgment itself is a consequence of *inductive reasoning*. Professor Diamond himself comes close to saying this, when he says that the truth of such propositions is grasped by "a kind of direct seeing or perception." But what that seeing or perception is, in virtue of which the equality of mankind is said to be a self–evident truth, Professor Diamond never tells us. It is vain to keep repeating that a self–evident truth has its truth within itself, without revealing *what that truth is*.

We will soon see that Professor Diamond hasn't the slightest idea of why—and in what sense—the truths proclaimed by the Declaration are true. To begin with, it is a manifest contradiction of the entire teaching of a Declaration addressed to "the opinions of mankind" and to a "candid world," to say that "these truths would not be self-evident to kings or nobles. . . ." This would imply that the judgments of the mind in respect of things whose evidence is immediately accessible to everyone, are determined by the social or political class of the observer. Such a doctrine is to be found in the writings of Karl Marx, but not in those of Thomas Jefferson. If it were true, we would not have found the Marquis de Lafayette among the ranks of the American revolutionaries. Professor Diamond falls into an even grosser historicism when he says that the "triumphant freedom" of the American Revolution would enable others to see and hold these truths to be self-evident. *Any* successful revolution will draw adherents in its wake, and most men will repeat the slogans of whatever political movement seems to be most powerful. The principles to which Jefferson appealed seem to have been more popular in the Paris of 1776—in the court of Louis XVI—than in the Paris of Jean Paul Sartre in 1976. Unlike the alleged truths of Marxism, which claim to predict the future, the *political* success or *political* failure of the American Revolution is utterly irrelevant to the *cognitive*—or moral—status of the truths proclaimed by Jefferson.

When Professor Diamond also says that Jefferson knew that "those truths had not hitherto been held as evident by the vast majority of mankind," he is also in error. In this case, the error is somewhat more subtle. Ten days before he died, Jefferson wrote:

The general spread of the light of science has already laid open to every view the palpable truth, that the mass of mankind has not been born with saddles on their backs, nor a favored few, booted and spurred, ready to ride them legitimately, by the grace of God.[91]

That the *natural* differences among men do not of themselves give *legitimacy* to the *political* differences, has in a certain sense always been known. Or, more precisely, it has been known as long as the idea of nature, and in particular of human nature, has been known. It certainly is as old as Stoicism, with its idea of a universal humanity, an idea which preceded Christianity in the Roman world by some centuries. According to Jefferson, spurious theories—of which the divine right of kings was his favorite example—have given "legitimacy" to non-natural or conventional differences. To illustrate Jefferson's thought by a familiar example: let the Prince and the Pauper change clothes unawares, and the Prince will become a Pauper, and the Pauper a Prince. The boys do not differ, it is only their clothes, and the theories that endow the clothes with seemingly magical properties. It is not objective difference in the boys, but subjective differences in the way others look at the boys, that cause the one to be called a Prince and the other a Pauper. The subjects of the Prince always knew that without his clothes he would look very much like any other boy of his age in an undressed condition. In that sense it was always evident to them that by nature the boys were equal, and that their actual inequality was conventional. The difficulty is to understand why they should have consented to conventions that would seem to endow the Prince, by virtue of his clothes, with a status in which he would appear as a being of a superior species. Such superstitions—for so Jefferson regarded them— Jefferson hoped would be dispelled by "the light of science." Then what all civilized men everywhere somehow always knew—namely, that by nature men are all equal in authority—would become the original and originating ground of political obligation.

Professor Diamond's analysis of the Declaration then continues:

> The Declaration holds certain truths to be self-evident: that all men are created equal, that they are endowed by their creator with certain unalienable rights among which life, liberty, and the pursuit of happiness, that governments, whose proper end is to secure these rights, may only be instituted by the consent of the governed, and that, when government becomes destructive of those rights, the people have the further right to alter

or abolish it and reinstitute another in its place. Now these truths do not rise by inference one from the other but are each equally and independently self-evident; and each is indispensably a part of a whole that forms the "sentiment" of the Declaration. Yet for our purpose tonight, and perhaps even intrinsically, we may single out as the most important political truth the comprehensive one regarding the institution of government, namely, that government exists to secure unalienable rights and must be instituted by popular consent. Thus men are created equal but only with respect to the equal possession of certain unalienable rights. Those rights give the content to and hence define our equality: what we are equally is equally free. But this equal freedom becomes, of course, political freedom, and hence politically interesting only under government. And, the final, self-evident truth, that is, the right to overthrow despotic government and reinstitute a new one, is obviously ancillary to the truth that deals with what legitimate government is and must do.[92]

Professor Diamond begins the foregoing paragraph by paraphrasing the statement of principles at the beginning of what he says is usually called the second paragraph of the Declaration. The paraphrase, in itself, is unobjectionable. But it is vitiated by the omission of any reference to the previous paragraph, and to Jefferson's assertion in it of "the laws of Nature and of Nature's God," under which the United States claim their "equal station." No interpretation of the Declaration which fails to link the God of Nature in the first paragraph with the Creator in the second, can succeed. Let us see.

The Declaration begins its assertion of principles declared to be self-evident with the proposition that all men are created equal. That proposition has a peculiar priority and independence from what follows it. Abraham Lincoln, in the Gettysburg Address, refers to the Declaration *only* by speaking of the nation as "conceived in liberty, and dedicated to the proposition that all men are created equal." To Lincoln the purpose of the Declaration seemed to be wholly embodied in the famous proposition, although liberty seems to have preceded it as conception precedes gestation and birth. Now if the truths of the Declaration do "not arise by inference one from another but are each equally and independently self-evident," then Lincoln must have been mistaken in the Gettysburg Address. For Lincoln clearly assumes that dedication to that one self-evident truth implied dedication to them all, and that dedication to them all implied as well dedication to "government of the people, by the people, for the people."

Professor Diamond admits that Jefferson, "as the author of the Declaration, had clearly drawn inspiration from John Locke." Let us then follow Locke in perhaps the most famous passage of the "Essay concerning the true original extent and end of civil government." We have given the title of Locke's work as Jefferson gave it, in his resolutions drawn for the Board of Visitors of the University of Virginia. There, we recall, Locke's book is given the first position among the works wherein are to be found "the general principles of liberty, and the rights of man, in nature and society." Locke considers "what state all men are naturally in." It is, he says,

> a state of perfect freedom to order their actions and dispose of their possessions and persons as they think fit, within the bounds of nature, without asking leave or depending upon the will of any other man.

But it is also, he continues,

> [a] state . . . of equality, wherein all the power and jurisdiction is reciprocal, no one having more than another; there being nothing more evident than [meaning that it is self-evident] that creatures of the same species and rank . . . should also be equal one amongst another without subordination and subjection. . . .[93]

We would re-phrase Locke's argument as follows: there is no difference between man and man, as there is between man and—for example—dog, such that one is recognizable as the other's *natural* superior. If then men are not naturally subordinate, one to another, as all brute creation is naturally subordinate to man, then men are not naturally in a state of government or civil society. They are instead naturally free and independent, or born free and independent. Being born free and independent, they are for that very reason born—or created—equal.

We see then that man's natural liberty, or his freedom and independence by nature, and his equality by nature, are mutual and reciprocal aspects of each other. Far from being independently self-evident, as Professor Diamond says, none are self-evident at all, *except* as reciprocal aspects of the same phenomenon. Professor Diamond says that "what we are equally is equally free." But he neglects the crucial qualification that—at least as far as Locke and the Declaration are concerned—this is true only by *nature*. Within civil society, the citizen on military duty is not equally as free as the citizen who is a civilian. The policeman who directs traffic—thereby inhibiting the equal freedom of motorists—does not have this authority from nature, but from the law of civil society. Without his uniform and badge—like the Prince and the Pauper—one could not distinguish him from those he directs. He would then merely be their equal, and they would be free to disregard his commands. Natural equality and natural freedom are then inseparable. Although they are distinguishable, they can no more be separated than the concavity and the convexity of a curved line.

But what of the other truths proclaimed as self-evident by the Declaration, that men are endowed by their Creator with the rights (among others) to life, liberty, and the pursuit of happiness? Man in the state of nature is under the law of nature. Concerning what that law is, we turn to James Madison, writing in the 43rd number of *The Federalist*. We observe that number 43 is the central number of that book. Madison's language here reminds us of the *first* paragraph of the Declaration—which Professor Diamond had omitted from his paraphrase. It is accordingly one of the direct links between the Declaration, James Madison, and the Constitution, links which Professor Diamond persistently denies. In recurring, says Madison, to "the absolute necessity of the case," we recur "to the great principle of self-preservation; to the transcendent *law of nature and of nature's God*."[94] This law dictates "that the safety and happiness of society are the objects at which all political institutions aim, and to which all such institutions must be sacrificed." In the state of nature, however, there are no political institutions. The great principle of self-preservation, the law of nature and of nature's God, there has reference to individuals. In the state of nature, man's right to self-preservation—his right to life—is the foundation of all else. His right to liberty follows from his right to life, because a man may not be rightfully denied the liberty of any action he thinks is necessary to preserve his life. If there were in the state of nature anyone who might rightfully tell him that he ought not to take a certain action to preserve his life, or who might tell him that he ought not to preserve his life by taking such an action, that would imply a natural inequality of human authority such as Locke, Jefferson, Madison, and the tradition of the Founders uniformly deny. But further: individuals in the state of nature must have a right to property.[95] For everyone, exercising his natural liberty, acquires and (within limits) accumulates food, clothing, shelter, and weapons. Without these—the necessary consequences of natural liberty—he could not preserve his life. Hence also the right to bear arms becomes an unalienable right, alongside of, as it is implied in, the right to property. Now the *exercise* of these unalienable rights may be modified and directed by civil society, once civil society is brought into existence by the social contract. But the social contract rests upon the assumption that the rights themselves are unalienable, and that they are possessed equally by all the parties who unanimously contract with each other to form civil society. The social contract transfers to the majority that executive power of the law of nature which each was entitled to—and obliged to—exercise for himself in the state of nature. The rights themselves form a continuum of inferences from man's natural equality.[96] It is the self-evidence of this equality which is the sole—but sufficient—ground for all man's natural rights. Contrary to Professor Diamond, none of these rights are "independently self-evident." Moreover, the unbroken chain of inference, connecting natural equality, with government by the majority of all who are parties to the social contract, connects the proposition of equality with government of, by, and for the people. Professor Diamond to the contrary notwithstanding, the Gettysburg Address rests upon a perfectly sound theoretical foundation.

By the logic of the Declaration, civil society is instituted for the security of men's unalienable rights. It is instituted to gain for those rights a security it is not possible for them to enjoy in the state of nature. But it is the exercise of these rights which is surrendered when men enter civil society, not the rights themselves. Nor is the exercise of all such rights surrendered. According to Jefferson, the rights of conscience, by which we determine our obligations to God, are not the business of civil society, and are not subject to regulation by that society. However, the security of man's unalienable rights—including the rights of conscience—is and remains the end for the sake of which any and every legitimate civil society is instituted. Hence the form of civil society, if it be legitimate, must be adapted to such ends. Hence we are brought to the following question: given the identity of purpose of every legitimate civil society, is there not some identity in the structure of every such society? We believe that the Declaration gives an affirmative answer to this question. Before presenting our own analysis of the text of the Declaration, we continue to its end the commentary of Professor Diamond, as presented in his Distinguished Lecture.

> What is especially interesting to us tonight [he continues], is the way this political truth of the Declaration has been transformed as it was formed and then absorbed into the historical American credo of government. We must read the Declaration closely to free ourselves from two centuries of obscuring usage. We have transformed the Declaration in our minds by reading the phrase "consent of the governed" as meaning rule by majorities, that is, democratic government. Indeed we think of the Declaration as our great democratic document, as the clarion call to and guide to our democratic nature. But the Declaration does *not* say that consent is the means by which the government is to operate. Rather, it says that consent is necessary only to institute the government, that is, to establish it.
>
> The people need not, then, *establish* a government which *operates* by means of their consent. In fact, the Declaration says that they may organize government on "such principles" as they choose, and they may choose "any form of government" they deem appropriate to secure their rights. That is, the Declaration was not prescribing any particular form of government at all, but was following John Locke's contract theory, which taught the right of the people, in seeking to secure their liberties, to establish *any* form of government. And by any form of government the Declaration emphatically includes—as any literate eighteenth century reader would have understood—not only the democratic form of government but also aristocratic and monarchical government as well. That is why, for example, the Declaration has to submit facts to a "candid world" to prove the British king guilty of a "long train of abuses." Tom Paine, by way of contrast, could dispose of King George more simply. Paine deemed George III unfit to rule simply because he was a *king* and kingly rule was illegitimate as such. The fact that George was a "Royal Brute" was only frosting on the cake; for Paine his being royal was sufficient warrant for deposing him. But the Declaration, on the contrary, is obliged to prove that George was indeed a brute. That is, the Declaration holds George III "unfit to be the ruler of a free people" not because he was a king, but because he was a tyrannical king. Had the British monarchy con-

tinued to secure to the colonists their rights, as it had prior to the long train of abuses, the colonists would not have been entitled to rebel. It was only the fact, according to the Declaration, that George had become a tyrannical king that supplied warrant for revolution.

Thus the Declaration, strictly speaking, is neutral on the question of forms of government; *any* form is legitimate provided it secures equal freedom and is instituted by popular consent [All emphasis by Professor Diamond].[97]

The foregoing completes the text of Professor Diamond's commentary.

Beneath the lucid surface of these comments lies confusion. On the one hand, Professor Diamond insists that it is the right of the people to choose any form of government. However, he also says that, but for the "long train of abuses," the American people would have had no right to rebel against the authority of the British crown. It is one thing to say that in such a case it would have been imprudent for them to rebel, but another to say that they would have had no right to do so.

A more profound error arises from Professor Diamond's assumption that, if the people may choose any form of government, therefore the Declaration is neutral with respect to forms of government. To say that the people may choose any form, is to say no more than that there is no authority above the people, to whom they are obligated to defer. It does not in the least imply that there are no criteria inherent in the nature of the people itself, by which their choice ought to be guided. Professor Diamond himself half recognizes this when he says that the people may choose any form of government, *provided* that it secures equal freedom and is instituted by popular consent. But is "equal freedom" equally the end of any and every form of government? Has not "equal freedom" been understood, at least since Plato and Aristotle, as peculiarly a democratic end. Among non-despotic regimes, has not wealth been understood to be the end of oligarchies, honor of monarchies, and virtue (however understood) of aristocracies? While it may be said that all non–despotic regimes preserve "equal freedom" in some degree, surely they do not do so in the same degree. Nor do all non–despotic forms of government recognize the need for popular consent in the institution of government. All stable governments, including stable despotisms, recognize the desirability if not the necessity for the consent of the government. The worst despotisms that the world has ever seen—those of Hitler and Stalin—invoked the principle of popular consent by means of the plebiscite. Something called consent may range all the way from the acquiescence of a slave, whose life has been spared by his master on the battlefield, to that of a free man deliberating with his equals, as to what they deem best for their common good. Regimes or forms of government vary greatly, both in the degree to which they conceive themselves as resting upon popular consent, and in the meaning that they give to the concept of popular consent. Hitler's and Stalin's regimes conceived of themselves as resting wholly and directly upon a foundation of popular consent, although the consent itself was a product, or by-product, of terror. The British constitution considers that sovereignty resides formally in the Queen in Parliament, not in the people as such. The consent of the governed, to the British government, is merely an inference drawn from the acceptance by the people of the mode by which Queen and Parliament are chosen. Even in the United States, where sovereignty is held to reside wholly in the people, the people have never been asked to act directly upon the question of the form of their government. Representative bodies, especially chosen for the purpose, ratified the Constitution in 1787. But the representativeness of those bodies is assumed rather than proved. There is then very little except the name in common between the popular consent which underlies the choice by the American people of their present form of government, and that given by Stalinist or Hitlerite plebiscites. All these distinctions drift into obscurity in Professor Diamond's facile conclusion that the Declaration authorizes any form of government, provided it secures equal freedom, and is instituted by popular consent.

We have seen that, according to Professor Diamond, the people "may choose 'any form of government' they deem appropriate. . . ." Taken in the abstract, this assertion is correct because, as we have noted, there is no authority above the people to deny their choice. However, the phrase "any form of government," taken from the Declaration, does not occur in the Declaration itself in the manner or place suggested by Professor Diamond. It occurs in the passage that reads thus: "whenever any form of government becomes destructive of these ends, it is the right of the people to alter or to abolish it. . . ." In such a case, the Declaration continues, the people have the right "to institute new government, laying its foundation on such principles and organizing its powers in such form, as to them shall seem most likely to effect their safety and happiness." Professor Diamond has then transferred "any form of government," from its place in the text, where it is the substantive object of "to alter and abolish," and made it appear as if it were the object of "to institute." He thus assumes that the right to alter or abolish any form of government is the same as the right to institute any form of government. But this is simply a *non sequitur*. Would anyone suppose that the right of a physician to alter or abolish any form of disease implies a right to institute "any form" of health? Has the multiplicity of the forms of evil ever been understood to imply a similar multiplicity in the forms of good? That men are originally—or by nature—equal, and that the natural ground of civil society is this equality, is easily forgotten in civil society. Moreover, it is easy for rulers to deceive both themselves and their subjects into thinking that they are inherently different and superior. It is easy to confuse the Prince's clothes—the customs or laws that endow him with authority—with his nature. That "frequent recurrence to fundamental principles," of which the Virginia Bill of Rights (June 12, 1776) so eloquently speaks, is needed precisely to remind the citizens, both governors and governed, of the natures which the instituted laws are meant to serve.

Because of natural equality, all government rests upon consent. But this consent varies greatly from government to government. When Jefferson wrote that the "just powers" of government are derived "from the consent of the governed," he was writing in an elliptical style. Although that style was perfectly clear to his contemporaries, the "obscuring usage" of two centuries, of which Professor Diamond writes, has unfortunately foreshortened his meaning. What Jefferson meant was that "just powers" arise from just or enlightened consent. Men who understand their natural equality or natural rights do not agree or consent to governments which do not secure their rights. Not consent as mere acquiescence of the will, but consent enlightened by full consciousness of natural rights, and by the aptness of governments to secure those rights, is consent in the full or proper meaning of the term. Men can hardly be "neutral" towards forms of government, unless they are neutral towards their own rights.

The second reference in the Declaration to instituting government refers especially to "new government." In the first reference we were presented with the inherent or just relationship between human equality, human rights, and human government. The significance of the "new" may be gathered in part from the references later in the Declaration to "barbarous ages" and to "merciless . . . savages." The people the Declaration represents, and the peoples to whom it is addressed, have emerged from a past characterized both by barbarism and savagery. The enlightenment, without which there is not true consent, has not always been present, nor is it everywhere present. Later it is asserted that the king is guilty of conduct "unworthy the head of a civilized nation," and that "our British brethren . . . have been deaf to the voice of justice and consanguinity." Barbarism is not only antecedent to civilization but is latent within it. But knowledge of "the laws of nature and of nature's God"—the true principles of civilization—are better understood now than hitherto. As George Washington wrote in 1783,

> The foundation of our empire was not laid in the gloomy ages of ignorance and superstition; but at an epocha when the rights of mankind were better understood and more clearly defined, than at any other period.[98]

Hence a people may now be presumed to be better able than before to institute a government which secures their rights. "New" government has better reason to be "good" government.

Let us remind ourselves of the precise words of the Declaration, in which the second reference to instituting government occurs.

> That whenever any form of government becomes destructive of these ends, it is the right of the people to alter or to abolish it, and to institute new government, laying its foundations on such principles and organizing its powers in such form, as to them shall seem most likely to effect their safety and happiness.

Professor Diamond, we have seen, interprets "such principles" and "such form" to mean *any* principles and *any* form, as if it were a matter of the mere pleasure of the people how they exercised their sovereign authority. This interpretation supports Professor Diamond's fundamental thesis, that "the Declaration . . . can offer no guidance whatsoever . . . for . . . American democratic institutions." The thought that shaped "American democratic institutions" is, he thinks, to be sought in the Constitutional Convention of 1787, but not in the Continental Congress from which the Declaration had emerged. We have already seen that James Madison actually said the opposite of what Professor Diamond represents him as saying, in his correspondence with Jefferson in 1825. But Madison had also expressed himself on this subject much nearer to the event, in the *Federalist* itself. In the 39th number, he had raised the question of whether the proposed new government "be strictly republican." "It is evident," he continued,

> that no other form would be reconcilable with the genius of the people of America; with the fundamental principles of the Revolution; or with that honorable determination which animates every votary of freedom, to rest all our political experiments on the capacity of mankind for self-government.[99]

We observe only that the central reason given why the government under the new Constitution had to be republican, was that "no other form would be reconcilable . . . with the fundamental principles of the Revolution." Can there be any doubt that those principles are to be found, above all, in the Declaration of Independence? According to James Madison then, in his most authoritative writing, the American commitment to democratic institutions is already complete in the Declaration of Independence.

At this point we would guard against misconstruction by reason of our substitution of the word "democratic" for "republican." For the Founding generation, "democracy" generally referred, as Madison says in the 14th *Federalist*, to a form in which "the people meet and exercise the government in person." In a republic, by contrast, "they assemble and administer it by their representatives and agents." "A democracy," he continues, "consequently, will be confined to a small spot." But a republic "may be extended over a large region."[100] For many and complex reasons—but partly because of the impossibility of any modern government being "exercised"

117

by the people "in person"—the name of democracy has been transferred to that form of government that the Founders called republican. We should also bear in mind that the strictures *against* democracy—as for example those in the 10th *Federalist*—are strictures against the direct government of the people, and *not* against the representative form of popular government that we now call democracy.

In asserting that the Declaration considers it the right of the people "to establish *any* form of government," Professor Diamond insists that this "emphatically includes—as any literate eighteenth century reader would have understood—not only the democratic form of government but also aristocratic and monarchical government as well." In stressing this point Professor Diamond draws a distinction between the opinions represented in the Declaration and those of Tom Paine. The former, he says, accept monarchy as a legitimate form of government, and for this reason Jefferson is obliged to prove, by the "long train of abuses," that George III was no longer a king but a tyrant. For Paine, Professor Diamond thinks, it was sufficient that George III was a king, to establish his illegitimacy. Let us then ask how—or in what sense—Jefferson regarded the British monarchy as legitimate.

A Summary View of the Rights of British America was written by Jefferson almost exactly a year before the Declaration of Independence. It is perhaps the most important single native source of Revolutionary ideas, anticipating most of the thoughts, and many of the actual phrases, of the Declaration itself. The *Summary View* takes the form of resolutions, recommended for adoption by the delegates to the Virginia Convention. The resolutions were never actually adopted as such, but their publication had an incalculable impact on opinion both in the colonies and in Great Britain.

The address to the throne, Jefferson writes,

> is penned in the language of truth, and divested of those expressions of servility, which would persuade his Majesty that we are asking favors, and not rights . . . and this his Majesty will think we have reason to expect when he reflects that he is no more than the chief officer of the people, appointed by the laws, and circumscribed with definite powers, to assist in working the

great machine of government, erected for their use, and, consequently, subject to their superintendance. . . .[101]

What kind of monarchy is it, in which "subjects" address the throne in such terms? One in which the king is no more than "chief officer of the people" and "subject to their superintendance?" How different is a king from a president, or monarchy from republicanism, so far as the theory of the two are concerned, from the point of view expressed here. It is true that Great Britain was then—as it is now—governed by (or rather with) an hereditary royal house. However, since the Glorious Revolution, the title to rule was founded in an act of Parliament, rather than hereditary right *per se*. From the radical Whig view—which Jefferson certainly represented—the Parliamentary title was the only one that counted. The fact that the people—through Parliament—chose their chief executive from a certain family, was merely incidental. In 1776, not all Britons were Whigs, much less radical Whigs. But very nearly all Americans, or all American who were not Tories, were so. In short, from the point of view of the Declaration, British monarchy was republicanism under the forms of monarchy. Today it is still a monarchy, yet no one doubts that it is, at the same time, a democracy. Tom Paine would also have accepted a monarch who was in substance if not in form a republican chief executive. In 1790 Jefferson was to write that: "The republican is the *only* form of government which is not eternally at open or secret war with the rights of mankind [Emphasis added]."[102] There can be no doubt that this point of view informed the Declaration of Independence as much as it did Jefferson's later, personal expression. This does not mean, however, that the Declaration did not envisage that a variety of forms of government—including a variety of forms of republicanism—might from time to time receive the people's sanction. For the Declaration includes a teaching in regard to *prudence*, which modifies the application of its teaching concerning *rights*.

By the Declaration the people, in instituting "new government" lay its foundations "on such principles" and organize its powers "in such form" as "to them shall seem most likely to effect their safety and happiness." Taken by itself, this would suggest that both principles and form are determined merely because of how they "seem" to the people. Yet the principles have already been stated, and they have been called self-evident truths. These truths are objective facts, and what *seems* to be true to the people must *be* true, if the powers of government are to be just. It is only the consent of an enlightened people that gives rise to the just powers of government; yet we must recognize that not all peoples are enlightened, nor are all enlightened to the same degree. Jefferson treated the British constitution as possessing greater legitimacy, as resting upon more enlightened opinion, before 1776, than he did afterwards. While himself a subject of the crown, he appealed prudently to its more enlightened elements, evidently hoping that by such an appeal he could strengthen those elements. Later, as an American citizen, he would treat the British constitution as radically defective. By then, he evidently hoped to widen the gulf between them, in favor of a more enlightened, or purer, republicanism here. With such considerations in mind, let us turn to the passage in the Declaration in which prudence is invoked.

> Prudence indeed will dictate that governments long established should not be changed for light or transient causes; and accordingly all experience hath shown, that mankind are more disposed to suffer, while evils are sufferable, than to right themselves by abolishing the forms to which they are accustomed.

Underlying this passage, we again emphasize, is the vision of a history of mankind, in transition from a barbarous age of ignorance and superstition, to one in which rights of man are better understood than ever before. In the course of this transition, the "moderate imperfections" of government, as Jefferson was to write in 1816, "had better be borne with. . . ." In part, this is because "we accomodate ourselves to them and find practical means of correcting their ill effects."[103] Consent may then actually be given to defective governments. By the very fact however that the Declaration speaks of the "evils" mankind suffers, it can hardly be thought indifferent towards the forms of government productive of those evils. It cannot be neutral towards different forms of government any more than it can be indifferent towards the difference between enlightenment on the one hand, and ignorance and superstition on the other. The greater the enlightenment of the people, the greater their inclination not merely towards *republican* government but, as we shall see, towards pure republican government. The Declaration recognizes that a people may accomodate themselves to a government less enlightened in its principles or in its form than they might wish, or than they ought to wish: for the power of custom may make the people sluggish in asserting their rights. But this in no sense constitutes neutrality in the teaching of the Declaration.

The argument of the Declaration of Independence requires that Jefferson demonstrate to the world that the action of the American people is not only *right* but that it is *prudent*. Because "mankind are more disposed to suffer while evils are sufferable," mankind may not sympathize with the actions of the Americans, unless the evils under which they suffer are believed to have become insufferable. While all light and transient evils are sufferable, it does not follow that all sufferable evils are light and transient. Evils that are deep-seated may nonethelesss be sufferable—or deemed sufferable— because of this deep–seated tendency of mankind *not* "to right themselves by abolishing the forms to which they are accustomed." The range of contingencies which might give rise to a range of legitimate—but varyingly imperfect—governments, is immense. The distinction between what is desirable, or acceptable, in a given set of circumstances, and what is desirable in itself, is however as firmly fixed in the Declaration of Independence as it is in Aristotle's *Politics*.

How deep–seated sufferable evils may be is shown by the "patient sufferance of these colonies." That patience extends to the margins of "absolute despotism" and "absolute tyranny." The charge against the crown is made of "a design to reduce [the people] under absolute despotism," and of a "direct object" to establish "an absolute tyranny over these states." The exact significance of distinguishing "despotism" over the people from "tyranny" over the states is not altogether clear. What is clear however is the comprehensiveness of the indictment, urging both the usurped and wrongful character of the authority (tyranny) and the debasement of free men to the character of slaves (despotism.) From both points of view however the wrongfulness and debasement are pronounced "absolute." If there are degrees of despotism or tyranny, to the milder forms of which men might sometimes submit, as to lesser evils— but towards which they would not thereby be neutral—this is not such an instance. Here right and duty coincide, and there can be no question of the wisdom of this people in acting as they do, because it is "necessity" which contrains them to alter their former systems of government.

Professor Diamond, in arguing that the Declaration is neutral towards forms of government, argues that "consent is necessary only to institute government." "The people," he says, "need not *establish* a government which *operates* by means of their consent."[104] This thesis he has repeated endlessly in a variety of lectures and articles. It has perhaps received its widest notoriety in his text-book, *The Democratic Republic* (Second Edition), wherein he labors the point as follows:

> We have transformed the Declaration by reading consent of the governed as rule by majorities, that is, democratic government. But the Declaration does not say that consent is the means by which government is to be *operated*; rather, consent is necessary only to *institute* the government, that is, to establish it.[105]

So persuasive has Professor Diamond been on this point, and so pervasive his influence, that we find Professor Edward C. Banfield, in his own Distinguished Lecture in this same series, echoing him. ". . . as Martin Diamond pointed out in his lecture in this series, the Declaration says that consent is required to institute or establish a government, not for the conduct of its affairs." To this, Professor Banfield adds that: "The unchallenged principle was that the conduct of affairs belonged in the hands of those authorized to govern."[106] In a footnote to this last sentence, Professor Banfield quotes Harvey C. Mansfield, Jr., to the effect that Jefferson was "willing to trust the people, not to govern, but to choose their governors."[107]

Now there can be no doubt that the democratic government favored by Jefferson was representative, and not the direct government of the people "in person." Strictly speaking, government "by majorities" would be possible only by the people "in person." In this sense—but only in this sense—Jefferson certainly did not have government by majorities in mind, either when he penned the Declaration, or thereafter. It is also certain, as Professor Mansfield maintains in the essay cited by Professor Banfield, that Jefferson hoped that the representatives authorized by the people to govern, would be as highly qualified as talents and education could make them. But any inference from this that the opinion of the governed was not to enter substantially into the operation of government, is wholly unwarranted.

It is unfortunate for Professor Diamond's argument, and for all those who have been influenced by that argument, that he did not take not of the fact that "consent" occurs not once, but three times in the Declaration. Its first occurrence does indeed refer primarily to the *institution* of government. But the second and third occurrence refer unmistakably and unequivocally to its *operation*. In the indictment of the King, Jefferson writes that

> He has kept among us, in times of peace, standing armies without the consent of our legislature.

And again, that the King has "combined with others," meaning the Parliament at Westminster, "giving his assent to their acts of pretended legislation." Among such acts are those

> For imposing taxes on us without our consent.

It is of paramount importance to notice the gradation in the three usages of "consent." The first, as we have said, refers on its face only to institution. The second refers to a distinct operation of government, but the consent required is to be given by "our legislature." In the third case, however, not only is it an operation of government which is involved, but the consent referred to, is not merely that of "our legislature." It is instead called "our consent." Nothing could be more deliberate or significant than this phraseology. Jefferson certainly intended that consent to taxes would, in fact, be given by representatives. But in consenting to taxation, the representatives were in a peculiar sense the instrument of the people themselves. For the "us" of "our consent" can be none other than "We the people."

Let us observe further that, while the quartering of troops is a singular operation of government, the raising of taxes is not. The peculiarly emphatic consent required for taxes, is then a peculiarly emphatic requirement for consent for all the operations of government for which taxes are necessary. For all practical purposes, this means all operations of government.

Further light on the meaning of the requirement of "our consent" is shed by Jefferson's *Summary View*. The most famous passage of that notable work is as follows.

> Still less let it be proposed that our properties within our own territories shall be taxed or regulated by any power on earth but our own. The God who gave us life gave us liberty at the same time; the hand of force may destroy, but cannot disjoin them.[108]

It will be noted that the great peroration, concerning God, life, and liberty, refers explicitly to the right to be taxed by no power but "our own." There is the same elision of expression here as there was to be, a year later, in the Declaration. Representatives do the taxing—and regulating—but only because they are "ours." But the *Summary View* makes explicit what is implicit in the Declaration: that the right to taxed only by "our consent" or by no other power but "our own" is a matter of *natural* right. It is not a mere incidence of British constitutionalism, or of that variant of British constitutionalism that had grown up in the colonies. The sequence of the rights to life, liberty, and the pursuit of happiness, is preceded in the foregoing passage of the *Summary View* by the rights to life, liberty, and the right not to have our properties taxed or regulated "by any power on earth but our own." A pure implementation of the principles of the Declaration of Independence—one unmediated by any prudential accommodation to circumstances—would then result in a purely republican—or democratic—form of government.

Professor Diamond has told us that "the issue of democracy was settled in this country by the drafting and ratification of the Constitution." However, as we have already argued, this would be true only if the issue of democracy and the issue of slavery were discrete and unrelated. We hold however with Abraham Lincoln, who said that there is no democracy where those who would not be slaves would not be masters. Yet it is remarkable that, in proclaiming the democratic character of the Constitution, Professor Diamond points to only one provision in it. This is "Article I, Section 2, which establishes the then broadest possible democratic franchise as the basis for the federal election."[109] We notice that Professor Diamond refers correctly to "*the* federal election," since election to the House of Representatives was the only election to any federal office, by the people themselves, required by the Constitution of 1787. In that Constitution, no popular election was necessary for Senate, for President or, of course, for federal judges or other federal officials. All the democracy to which Professor Diamond can point is comprised in the fact that the electors in each state for the House of Representatives "shall have the qualifications requisite for electors of the most numerous branch of the state legislature." In point of fact, the Constitution of 1787 is much more democratic than this sparse and inconclusive evidence suggests. Professor Diamond should have noticed that Representatives are chosen only for two years, making them peculiarly dependent upon those who elect them. But he should also have noted that in Article I, Section 7, it is declared that "All bills for raising revenue shall originate in the House of Representatives; but the Senate may propose or concur with amendments as on other bills." It is this constitutional priority of the House of Representatives in matters of taxation that makes the Constitution of 1787 notably democratic. For priority in raising revenue is equally priority in determining how it shall be spent. The right of the Commons to withhold supplies from the Crown is the central fact of English constitutional development, as it is also the historical precedent underlying this feature of the American Constitution. It is then the proximity of the revenue raising function to the people that makes the Constitution as it emerged from the Philadelphia Convention democratic, however indirect the role of the people may have been with respect to all its other functions. We have seen that, according to no less a witness than James Madison, no government that was not "strictly republican" would have been reconcilable with the principles of the Revolution—and hence with the principles of the Declaration. In 1816, Jefferson was to write that

> a government is republican in proportion as *every* member composing it has his *equal voice* in the direction of its concerns (not indeed in person, which would be impracticable beyond the limits of a city, or small township, but) by representatives chosen by himself, and responsible to him at short periods [Emphasis added].[110]

In 1854 Abraham Lincoln was to echo this sentiment, in his first great anti–slavery speech, calling for the restoration of the Missouri Compromise.

Allow ALL the governed an equal voice in the government, and that, and that only, is self-government [Emphasis by Lincoln].[111]

In this passage, Lincoln refers distinctly to slaves, no less than free citizens, as among the "governed." In this also he is echoing that remarkable passage from the *Notes on Virginia*, in which Jefferson calls the slaves "one half the citizens!" The phrase "equal voice," moreover, as used by both Jefferson and Lincoln, implies more than mere voting. It carries the connotation of such an influence upon the operations of government as is consistent with the idea of that influence passing through the medium of representatives. This does not in the least suggest that the representative do not have a constructive role, that they do not enlarge, refine, and qualify the influence whose medium they are. Above all they must enlighten— and sometimes infuse with wisdom—the influence they represent, even as they represent it. But what Jefferson wrote in 1816 and Lincoln repeated in 1854—and repeated again in 1863 at Gettysburg—is firmly grounded in the Declaration of Independence, just as the Declaration is itself firmly grounded in the *Summary View*. The American political tradition was radically democratic, as Lincoln said it was even from the moment of its conception. Amid the many spurious claimants that have arisen in the last two hundred years, it alone can rightly claim the title deeds to democracy rightly understood in the modern world. The man who more than any other was the progenitor of this tradition—whose principles Lincoln called "the definitions and the axioms of free society"[112]—was Thomas Jefferson. One can hardly imagine a greater disservice to the cause of perpetuating this tradition, than to obscure this fact.

Clinton Rossiter has written that "the hard core of the American tradition is a belief in constitutional government." When "the American pledges his allegiance to democracy," he continues,

he means *constitutional* democracy, a system of government in which political power is diffused by a written constitution and the wielders of power are held in check by the rule of law. In his opinion, there is no inherent conflict between democracy and constitutionalism . . . "constitutionalism" strengthens rather than frustrates the democratic process.[113]

We would go further than Rossiter, insisting that modern

democracy, properly so called *is* a constitutional process. We would deny that the good name of democracy should ever be conceded to any form of government in which the rule of the people is divorced from the rule of law. We would take issue with Tocqueville's thesis, that the principle of equality can lead either to despotism or to freedom. Only the principle of equality *wrongly understood* can lead to despotism. The true principle of equality, as propounded in the Declaration of Independence, and as reaffirmed in the Gettysburg Address, is indissolubly connected to a form of government in which those who make the law live under the law. We now live in a world in which regimes founded upon the plebiscite claim the authority of the people, and the name of democracy. No matter what such regimes call themselves, we should never concede to them the right that is properly that of a free people. For the authority of a free people can never give rise to any system of arbitrary power.

We have seen that Professor Diamond, in his account of the phrase "consent of the governed" has thoroughly misunderstood the concept of "consent" in the Declaration as a whole. He failed to perceive that consent to the operation of government is as much a requirement of natural right as is consent to the institution of government. However much circumstances or prudence may limit the implementation of natural right does not affect the intrinsic character of natural right itself. However, Professor Diamond was entirely correct in asserting that "consent of the governed" in the second paragraph in itself referred solely to the institution of government. But the distinction and difference between the consent required for *institution* and the consent required for *operation* underlies the distinction and difference between the authority of the people in making a *constitution*, and that in operating a *government*. One of the greatest American contributions to the science of government, has been the clear distinction between statute law, and constitutional law. The idea of the rule of law, as it developed in and through the American Founding, required that there be a written law, above the power of the ordinary powers of government, and by which the latter were defined and limited.

The idea of separation of powers is accompanied by the collateral—but distinct—idea of checks and balances. But neither of these is or can be fully effective, except in the light of the distinction between the legislative power as constituent, and the legislative power as ordinary. In British constitutionalism these two concepts emerged over the centuries as distinct, but they have never had any separate institutional embodiment. Yet in the United States, the idea of constitutional law being sanctioned by a legislative process distinct from that by which ordinary law was sanctioned, has been present from the beginning. Its presence is represented in the Declaration of Independence by the clear distinction between the consent required for the institution of government, and that required for its operation. Upon that distinction arose the American practice of convening extraordinary bodies, specially chosen for the purpose, from the body of the people, to ratify constitutional enactments. That is how the Constitution of 1787 was ratified. Even in 1860–1861, the seceding states, in deference to this principle, called what were in effect de-ratifying conventions. Claiming as they did the right of secession as a *constitutional* right, they proceeded constitutionally to implement it. In the course of American history, state constitutions have been submitted to a direct vote of the people, as distinct from ratifying conventions. The Constitution of 1787, which in this respect remains unchanged, allows different ways for both initiating and ratifying amendments to the fundamental law. The mode by which all amendments have in fact been ratified, has been by three–fourths of the state legislatures, of proposals by two–thirds of both houses of the Congress. Although ordinary legislative bodies are utilized in this process, the extraordinary conjunction of state and national legislatures required to give it effect, are understood to make the mode of amending the Constitution an exercise of the constituent legislative power by the people, and not of the ordinary legislative power of the government.

The constituent legislative power, we repeat, is the mode by which the people determine how they shall be governed, by consenting to government. Yet the "people" who do the consenting are not, in the case of the United States, a mere aggregate. They are the people as distributed in the several states. In the amending clause of the Constitution—Article V—it is provided that no state, without its consent, shall be deprived of its equal suffrage in the Senate. This guarantees the role of the states, not only in the ordinary legislative process, but in the amending process as well. In my opinion, it ought to continue to guarantee the role of the states in electing the President, as is done by the electors chosen for that purpose separately by the several states. It is an unsettled question in American constitutional law, whether or not an amendment might do away with any limitation upon the power of amendment. The concept of a people, in the American political tradition, is the concept of a civil polity constituted by unanimous consent, acting by a majority. This is reflected in the Constitution of 1787 by the provision that it shall come into effect, only between the states ratifying it; that is, by unanimous consent. Changes thereafter might be made, by three–fourths of the states. Not only must majorities for constituent purposes be *extraordinary* but they must be *distributed.* "We the people" act in our constituent capacity only as members of *states*, as majorities of majorities.

Edward S. Corwin's classic essay, "The 'Higher Law' Background of American Constitutional Law" begins as follows.

> The Reformation superseded an infallible Pope with an infallible Bible; the American Revolution replaced the sway of a king with that of a document.[114]

Yet in what follows, Corwin shows that the sway of the document came in time to be regarded as something like that of a king. We recall that Professor Kristol, in his Distinguished Lecture, invited us to ignore Tom Paine. Professor Corwin notes however that "the electrifying proposal that America should declare her independence from Great Britain" which appeared in *Common Sense*, was accompanied by another proposal in which Paine also "urged . . . a 'Continental Conference'. . . ." According to Corwin, "This suggestion . . . was to eventuate more than a decade later in the Philadelphia Convention. . . ."[115] The passage from *Common Sense* quoted by Corwin reads as follows:

> The conferring members being met, let their business be to frame a Continental Charter, or Charter of the United Colonies; (answering to what is called the Magna Charta of England) fixing the number and manner of choosing members of congress and members of assembly . . . and drawing the line of business and jurisdiction between them: (always remembering

that our strength is continental, not provincial) securing freedom and property to all men . . . with such other matter as it is necessary for a charter to contain. . . . But where, say some, is the King of America? Yet that we may not appear to be defective even in earthly honors, let a day be solemnly set apart for proclaiming the charter; let it be brought forth placed in the divine law, the word of God; let a crown be placed thereon, by which the world may know, that so far as we approve of monarchy, that in America the law is King.

The proposal that the "Continental Charter" be a kind of Magna Charta, securing the freedom and property of all men, certainly contains, in however rudimentary form, the considerations which led first to the Annapolis, and then to the Philadelphia Conventions. But Paine's identification of the rule of the people with the rule of law, and the rule of law with the rule of a King as representative of divine law, leads us to the most profound symbolism of the American political tradition.

It is commonly said that the voice of the people is the voice of God. But this saying is ambiguous. Is the name of God to be placed in the service of whatever the people may will in his name? Or is the will of the people to be subjected to such canons of reason and of justice as may properly be regarded as divine? In short, is such a saying an elevating of the people, or a lowering of the divine? Jefferson always regarded the *lex majoris partis* to be "sacred," but it was so in a most particular sense. In his first inaugural address, he spoke as follows.

> All, too, will bear in mind this sacred principle, that though the will of the majority is in all cases to prevail, that will, to be rightful, must be reasonable; that the minority possess their equal rights, which equal laws must protect, and to violate which would be oppression.[116]

How to reconcile the will of the majority with the *equal* rights of the minority, this is the peculiar task of popular government. But the will of the majority is sacred, not only because it is the greater *will*, but because it is informed by a process that is *reasonable*. Every word of this great passage from Jefferson's inaugural address is itself informed by the doctrine of the higher law derived from the Declaration, by which the ordinary operations of government take place under the aegis of a constitutional order itself beyond the ordinary means of popular control. And when the people exert themselves in their unique constituent capacity, it is never to reach the ordinary subjects of legislation, or objects of administration, but rather to lay down the processes whereby majority rule may be infused with reason, and the rights of the minority secured.

If we turn again to the text of the Declaration, we find not only a distinction between the consent required for the institution of government, and the consent required for its operation, but a corresponding distinction within the divine nature as well. First, there is a three-personed—or perhaps we should say a three–powered–God, who first appears in connection with the "laws of nature and of nature's God." In relationship to these laws of nature, this same God is also the "Supreme Judge of the world." And finally, for those who are faithfully obedient to these laws, he is the "Divine Providence" upon whom "firm reliance" may be placed. We see by this that constitutionalism and the rule of law, as represented by the principle of the separation of powers, is anticipated in the divine government of the universe.[117] We may also say that the unitary substance of God is manifested in three distinctly different aspects of that substance, for the perfection of that government. In like manner, all the just powers of government originate in the people—the equal individuals formed by unanimous consent into civil society. The substance of "the people," like that of God, is unitary; but the powers of the people's government must nonetheless be divided and separated, one from the other, for the perfection of the structure of that government. Yet the unity of the people is not natural, even when it is accomplished according to the laws of nature. It is a synthetic whole, while the unity of God is accomplished *a priori*: no social contract is necessary in order for God to be one. Because then God has no interest opposed to his interest— he cannot be unjust to himself—he can be simultaneously one and three. The same God may, under his different aspects or functions, legislate, judge, and execute, without any conflict of interest arising from a diversity within himself. But the people, although by law one, remain a composition of naturally discrete individuals, whose passions, notably as members either of a majority or a minority, are seldom in harmony with each other. Hence the individual persons who compose the legislative, judicial, and executive powers of human government, must (unlike God) be really different. The unity of God guarantees that his passion and his reason are in permanent and indissoluble harmony with each other: his reason is unaffected—that is, undistorted—by desire. In the case of the people's government however the social contract or law which makes the people one, must also make it three, or represent it in government by three distinct and separated powers.

The three personed God corresponding to the differentiated functions of government may be distinguished however from the originating Deity denominated as Creator. This God "endows" mankind with "certain unalienable rights." Without that endowment, and apart from that endowment, mankind would not only not have these rights, but its relationship with God and all of Creation would be different. We need not speculate upon whether another universe is possible, to see that the perfection of this universe corresponds with a "great chain of being" in which the lower natures are linked with the higher natures. Man remains lord of Creation, but his lordship arises from the fact that he, alone of created beings, is conscious of the whole, is open to the whole, of which he is a part. Man can by his thought grasp the principle of the whole and can thereby actualize the whole within himself. He thus becomes a microcosm mirroring the macrocosm. Man's unalienable rights are *a priori* self–evident truths. A truth, consciousness of which is as such a product of pure theoretical reason, becomes a right, a principle of practical reason, and of morally correct action. Truth and right, thought and action, God and man, higher and lower, macrocosm and microcosm, inform each other, and by so doing contribute to the perfection of the whole.

The God who is Creator, who endows man with his rights, is author of a universe whose excellence lies in the mutually reinforcing harmony of its parts or aspects or functions. By making the truths which are also rights "self-evident" the God who has created reveals the perfection or completion of his work. In the theological disputations of the middle ages, it was long a question whether God could have made a universe better than this one. According to one school of disputants, to say that God could not have made a better universe was heresy, because it would imply that God's power was limited.

But according to another school, to say that this universe was imperfect, would be heresy, because it would cast doubt upon the goodness of God. In the Declaration of Independence, this dispute is resolved by making power and goodness reciprocal. That "firm reliance" upon Divine Providence with which the Declaration of Independence concludes, in virtue of which the Signers pledge to each other their lives, fortunes, and sacred honor, is the same as the faith with which Lincoln, in 1860, concluded his address at Cooper Institute. "Let us," he exhorted his audience, "have faith that right makes might, and in that faith, let us, to the end, dare to do our duty as we understand it."[118] The understanding, of course, flowed from the self–evident truths of the Declaration, the truths which constituted the laws of nature, the laws which in their turn had been the work of a beneficent Creator.

The God of Creation, is a God whom we admire and praise; but above all is he a God whom we honor by acting rightly in accordance with the rights with which he had endowed us. The three–personed –or three–powered–God of nature is himself a result of Creation, as much as is man. He is bound by the laws of nature as is mankind. As supreme judge of the world, for example, he judges the rectitude of intentions. That is to say, he inquires into the question of whether, in assuming a separate and equal station, we do indeed intend to act in accordance with the rights with which the Creator has endowed us. God as judge, judges according to the laws of nature, the laws which are in accordance with our natural rights. What our intentions *ought* to be is a settled matter, as it is for any judge who interprets a law emanating from proper legislative authority.

In considering the dual character of the people, we must see them first as the "creator" of the legal order of human government. As such, we see that they too must, having once exerted their constituent—or creative—function, in establishing the constitutional legal order, recede from that order. They must establish the rules under which the government must operate: first, by enabling the government to secure the rights of the governed; and second, by so contriving the powers of government that the government may not itself become dangerous to the rights it exists to secure. But the exertions of the people in their constituent capacity must not usurp

133

the functions of government. The people as constituent, like the Creator, must not attempt to govern. But neither must government usurp constituent or constitution making functions. The three–personed–God of nature, governing the created universe, has no power to alter the Creation, the laws of nature, itself. Of course, the people as constituent cannot expect their work to be perfect once and for all, as is that of the Creator. Yet they must be aware of the need for identifying perfection with ultimate authority, and they must realize that frequent changes in fundamental law derogates from that sense of its excellence that contributes to its proper functioning. When James Madison in the 49th *Federalist* took issue with Jefferson for proposing a mode of amendment which might result in too frequent changes in fundamental law, he was offering a criticism founded in Jefferson's own thought. Yet Jefferson was not wrong in supposing with Washington that the rights of man were better understood than hitherto, and that perforce the relationship of human to divine government was also better understood. Surely as he reflected upon the stubborn attachment to slavery of his fellow-countrymen, Jefferson was not wrong in supposing that improvements might be made in the future as they had in the past. Yet neither he nor any of the Founders imagined that, two centuries after independence, the general understanding of the rights of man would have declined more precipitately than it had ever arisen.[119] Nor would they have supposed that universal barbarism, rather than further progress, should seem the more likely fate. We may say that they laid the foundations of a reasoned conservatism more necessary than they knew.

The people as creator of the constitutional order of government must not themselves attempt to govern, any more than does the Creator of the order of nature in the universe. As the latter leaves this task to the triune God, the people as constituent must leave the operating of government to the legislative, executive, and judicary powers. The people who participate in government are moulded and restrained by the laws of the constitutional creation. The constituent function never reaches particular cases, and as such it can never be unjust. Actual government always decides the fate of particular interests, or of groups of particular interests. But it does so, under a true constitution, under rules that minimize the possibility of arbitrariness. The judiciary, like the Supreme Judge of the world, looks to its order of its creation—the Constitution—for guidance. The doctrine of judicial review is a simple inference—or transference—from the relationship of Creation to institution under the laws of nature. The "Supreme Judge of the World" is a model for and anticipation of the Supreme Court of the United States.

The three powers of government are then symbolically present in the Declaration of Independence as aspects of that God in the Declaration who results from Creation, and who is the pattern and support for government in agreement with the rights of man. But the doctrine of the separation of powers is also present throughout the indictment of the British King and Parliament. The first large group of charges refers to unwarranted interferences or abuses of executive power in relationship to the legislative powers of the people. Another set of charges concern the interferences of the King with the independence of the judiciary. In charging that the King has "affected to render the military independent of and superior to the civil power," the Declaration is of course charging him with at once collapsing all three powers into one, and abolishing all dependence of the government upon the governed. Once the sword is independent of the purse, the robe—and all other functions of government—fall under the sword. The executive then ceases to be an executive "of the laws of nature." If not even God may govern his Creation except by laws, neither may a King—or a people. In the Declaration of Independence the identification of popular government with the rule of law is perfect and complete. Tom Paine was never more prescient, nor more in harmony with the doctrine of Thomas Jefferson, than when he wrote that in America there should be no king but the law. Nevertheless, the law *should* be King, as much as—and for the same reason as—God should be King of Kings.

According to Professor Diamond, the Declaration of Independence contained little more than a vague and undefined commitment to "equal freedom." We have seen however that it embraces not only the political but the constitutional principles of the American political tradition. Indeed, we have seen that no separation of political from constitutional principles is possible, in the teaching of the Declaration. We have seen that the Declaration is indeed a democratic document, conceiving all authority to be derived from the people, under the "laws of nature and of nature's God." But the very nature which makes the people sovereign requires the strict distinction of their constituent function from their governing function, of constitutional law from ordinary law. The Declaration favors democratic government above every other form of government, while recognizing the legitimacy of prudential accommodations to less than purely democratic forms. But the rule of the people in a democracy is not a rule according to the people's pleasure; it is a rule under the laws that the people in their constituent or "Creator" function have given themselves. The people rule under the laws of the constitutional order, as much as the God of nature rules under the laws of the Creator. Among the laws of the constitution, none is more fundamental than that providing for the separation of powers. The principle of separation of powers is clearly embodied in the Declaration. Yet it cannot be said that the means of implementing separation of powers was as well known in 1776, as it was by the time the Constitution of 1787 was drafted in Philadelphia.

The problem of the re-shaping of republicanism (or democracy) in the period of the Founding has been characterized with consummate learning by Professor Edward S. Corwin, in an essay published in 1925, entitled "The Progress of Constitutional Theory Between the Declaration of Independence and the Meeting of the Philadelphia Convention."[120] It is the thesis of that essay that the problem faced by the Convention was not to be understood merely as that of providing a national government stronger than that of the Articles of Confederation. The task of the Convention was equally—perhaps even more—that of providing a truer republicanism in the states severally, as well as in the nation. The problem of a democratic republicanism was stated long before the 10th *Federalist*, in the *Politics*, when Aristotle asks "For suppose the poor, because of their numbers, divide up the property of the rich, would this not be unjust?" A spokesman for democracy replies "It is done justly by the ruling authority, by Zeus!" To which the further reply is made,

"What else can be pronounced the extreme of injustice?"[121] This classic reproach to, and objection to democratic government, was precisely the heart of the difficulty of American republicanism in the Confederation period. Although state after state *declared* that the principle of separation of powers was to be observed, and that this was the foundation of the rule of law, the practice did not live up to the theory. In practice, the legislatures dominated both executive and judiciary. Sometimes private disputes concerning property were decided not by judges and juries, but by acts passed by majorities in popularly elected legislatures. "Popularity" and hence the idea of government by the people, sometimes took on the vicious meaning represented in the *Politics*. Nothing reveals the intentions of the Framers better than the prohibition upon the states in the Constitution, of the impairment of the obligation of contracts, and of the coining of money. Nothing destroyed property more capriciously and irresponsibly than voting the issuance of paper money. A majority of debtors could in effect divide up the property of their debtors, and could destroy the substance of the contracts between creditors and debtors, by demanding that their elected representatives vote for such measures. But this was not the rule of law, nor was it popular government as understood by Thomas Jefferson.

Professor Diamond we recall congratulated Divine Providence for keeping Jefferson out of the country during the meeting of the Philadelphia Convention, because he was "too easily given to a mere libertarianism that would have vitiated the effectiveness of government." It is not easy to assign precise meaning to these words. We know however from Professor Diamond's accounts elsewhere of the work of the Convention, that implementing the principle of separation of powers by checks and balances was central to that work. There was no attempt at separation of powers in the government of the Articles of Confederation, nor was there any apparent need for it. The fewness of its powers, and the dependence upon the states for the exercise of those few, made it seem superfluous. But a government with as many powers as the proposed government, and with the exercise of such powers bearing directly upon the citizens without any intervention by the states, changed everything. It was well understood by the authors of the *Federalist*, that the new government would never be accepted unless the ratifiers were satisfied that separation of powers would be implemented in such a way as to make those powers safe. It is notable then that Madison, in setting forth both this problem and its solution, in the 48th *Federalist*, should turn to Jefferson, in the *Notes on Virginia*, for authority and guidance. The passage which follows was quoted in full by Madison, in the text of the *Federalist*. The emphasis in the passage is, in the first instance, by both Jefferson and Madison. In the subsequent instances, it is by Madison alone. We remark in passing, that this same passage in the *Notes* is cited by Professor Corwin, as a classic analysis of the defects of government in the Confederation period, and hence a major milestone on the way that led to the Philadelphia Convention.

> All the powers of government [of the Revolutionary state Constitution of Virginia], legislative, executive, and judiciary, result to the legislative body. The concentrating these in the same hands, is precisely the definition of despotic government. It will be no alleviation, that these powers will be exercised by a plurality of hands, and not by a single one. One hundred and seventy–three despots would surely be as oppressive as one. Let those who doubt it, turn their eyes on the republic of Venice. As little will it avail us, that they are chosen by ourselves. An *elective despotism* was not the government we fought for; but one which should not only be founded on free principles, but in which the powers of government should be so divided and balanced among several bodies of magistracy, as that no one could transcend their legal limits, without being checked and restrained by the others. For this reason, that convention which passed the ordinance of government, laid its foundation on this basis, that the legislative, executive, and judiciary departments should be separate and distinct, so that no one person should exercise the powers of more than one of them at the same time. *But no barrier was provided between these several powers.* The judiciary and the executive members were left dependent on the legislature for their subsistence in office, and some of them for their continuance in it. If, therefore, the legislature assumes executive and judiciary powers, no opposition is likely to be made; nor, if made, can be effectual; because in that case they may put their proceedings into the form of acts of Assembly, which will render them obligatory on the other branches. They have accordingly, *in many* instances, *decided rights* which should have been left to *judiciary controversy*, and *the direction of the executive, during the whole time of their session, is becoming habitual and familiar.*[122]

This trenchant analysis, as Madison observes, was supported by

Jefferson's own experience as a war–time governor of Virginia, under the constitution he is criticising. But the author of the Declaration of Independence, better perhaps than anyone else, knew not only what the people of the United States, and of Virginia, were fighting against, in the Revolution, but what they were fighting *for*. And it was *not* an "elective despotism." That the government should have been popular did not in the least, in Jefferson's opinion, derogate from the possibility that it could be despotic. Jefferson, no less than Madison, considered a "dependence upon the people" unaccompanied by adequate "auxiliary precautions" to be an insufficient barrier to despotism or tyranny.

We are so accustomed now to think of separation of powers and checks and balances together, that it is difficult to grasp the fact that the doctrine of the one preceded the other by some time. In the perception of the necessity of checks and balances to implement separation of powers, Jefferson was one of the first. This statement in the *Notes* was certainly a powerful impetus to some of the most creative work of the Convention. Certainly no praise can be too high for Madison's subtle argument, that in permitting a *partial agency* of one branch in the powers of another, precisely that checking and balancing might be accomplished. As in other cases, Madison turned an argument against the Constitution—in this case the argument that it did not sufficiently separate the powers of government—into an argument for it. In the precise manner of providing this partial agency, the new Constitution brought the art of checking and balancing—and with it the art of the rule of law—to a new perfection. But in so doing, it was only implementing further the fundamental principles laid down before in the Declaration of Independence.

How to combine popular government with constitutional government and the rule of law, majority rule with minority rights, the common good with the personal freedom of each, these are problems that can never be solved once and for all. Their solution must be sought again and again, as new difficulties arise to challenge old answers. The Constitution itself, however, Professor Diamond to the contrary notwithstanding, does not set forth the principles it is designed to embody. There is nothing in the Constitution itself, to distinguish its perfections, from its compromises with perfection. At this point, we turn back to our beginning, to the Declaration itself, and to Abraham Lincoln's meditation upon the Declaration, in its relationship to the Constitution and the Union. Once again, we quote *Proverbs*, 25: 11.

A word fitly spoken is like apples of gold in pictures of silver.

According to Lincoln, the word fitly spoken, the apple of gold, to which we have devoted so much of our attention, was the assertion of principle in the Declaration of Independence. The pictures of silver are the Union and the Constitution subsequently framed around it. The pictures, said Lincoln, were "made *for* the apple—*not* the apple for the picture." "So let us act," he continued, "that neither *picture* or *apple*, shall ever be blurred, or broken."[123]

The danger that the picture might be broken is perhaps not so great—or at least so immediate—as it was in Lincoln's time. That the "apple of gold" might be blurred; or rather that it is blurred almost to the point of complete obscurity, is the great point of danger for us. Yet the obscurity lies not in the subject, but in us. If "we the people" do not know why we are a people, we cease to be one.

IV. Equality, Justice, and the American Revolution: In Reply to Bradford's "The Heresy of Equality"

"LET US HAVE no foolishness indeed," writes Professor Bradford, in his reply to "Equality as a Conservative Principle," echoing my echo of Willmoore Kendall:*

> Equality as a moral or political imperative, pursued as an end in itself—Equality, with the capital "E"—is the antonym of every legitimate conservative principle.[1]

In *The Federalist*, No. 51, Madison writes that "Justice is the end of government. It is the end of civil society. It ever has been and ever will be pursued until it be obtained, or until liberty be lost in the pursuit."[2] But what is justice? Let me enter into the record of our differences a passage from the *Nicomachean Ethics* which I would hope Professor Bradford might accept as canonical. In Book V, Chapter 3[3] both the unjust man and the unjust action are said to be unequal. Every action admitting more or less, says Aristotle, admits

---

*"The Heresy of Equality: Bradford Replies to Jaffa," *Modern Age*, Vol. 20, No. 1, Winter, 1976, pp. 62–77. The original title of Professor Bradford's essay, which he was kind enough to send me in typescript, was "Black Republicanism Redivivus: A Reply to Harry Jaffa." I greatly regret the change of title. Professor Bradford and I are carrying on a debate which reached a climax in the 1850's. His original title accurately indicates the political character of our differences. In applying to me the appelation that belonged above all to Abraham Lincoln, he has paid me a compliment that, however undeserved, I cannot forgo. As Professor Bradford explains in a note to his *Modern Age* essay, he is replying to my "Equality as a Conservative Principle," originally published in the *Loyola of Los Angeles Law Review*, VIII, (June, 1975), and now Chapter II of the present volume. As Professor Bradford correctly notes, "Lincoln's reading of the Declaration of Independence is the central subject of this entire exchange." But see also "Time on the Cross: Debate," in *National Review*, March 28, 1975, pp. 340–342, and 359. Here Bradford and I crossed swords for the first time.

also of a mean, which is the equal. "If then," he continues, "the unjust is the unequal, the just is the equal."

Aristotle divides justice into two kinds. The one, the justice that is in exchanges. The other, the justice that is in distributions either of honors or profits. As an example of the first kind, consider an exchange of shoes for grain. Somehow the quantity of shoes exchanged for a quantity of grain must be made equal. A common measure is needed, such as money. The shoes and the grain should then both be valued by the same amount of money. If they are so valued—things equal to the same thing being equal to each other— then the transaction may be said to be just. As an example of the second kind of justice, consider the honors or prizes awarded at the end of a race. The first place prize should go to the first place finisher, and the second place prize to the second place finisher. Or, 1/1 equals 2/2. The first kind of justice—in exchanges—is an equality of number: ten dollars worth of shoes equals ten dollars worth of grain. The second kind of justice—in distributions—is an equality of proportion. In both cases, however, the just is a species of the equal.

Equality is a conservative priciple because justice is conservative, and equality is the principle of justice. Where exchanges are just— that is, where one party does not overreach the other—and where distributions are just—that is, where rewards are proportioned to merit—men tend to become friends. Where the opposite is the case, they tend to become enemies. In Book V of the *Politics*[4] Aristotle declares that the most general or universal cause of *stasis* (faction or sedition) is inequality. Inequality—whether numerical or proportional—tends to disrupt and destroy political communities, and equality tends towards their harmony and their preservation. Equality as the ground of justice is then both good in itself and good for its consequences.

In the course of my praise of equality I had referred to a New Conservatism, properly so called, as being identical with the Old Liberalism, which was in my view the Liberalism of the Founding Fathers of the American regime. For the Liberalism of the Founders, in my understanding, was not merely that of locally disaffected British Whigs. Once the separation from the British crown was decided upon, they set out to build a new and more radically just political order than had existed in practice in any antecedent model. It was indeed intended to be the *novus ordo seclorum*, the new order of the ages, announced on the great seal of the United States. It was to decide, as Hamilton announced in the first *Federalist*, whether "societies of men [might be] capable of establishing good government [by] reflection and choice," or whether mankind was forever destined "to depend for their political constitutions on accident and force." From the perspective of the American founding, all previous governments, including that of Great Britain, however excellent some of their features, did not embody that reasonableness implied in the human capacity for "reflection and choice."[5] But the American founding was intended to do just that. The rule of priests and kings, and of priestly kings, and the legal privileges of hereditary orders generally, were regarded by our Founders as elements of unjust inequality in all European constitutions, including the British. The forbidding of the issuance of patents of nobility, either by the States or by the United States, the prohibition of any religious test for office, the absence of any property qualification for office, in the Constitution of 1787, all attest the revolutionary thrust against inequality. So does the prohibition of slavery in the great Northwest Ordinance, which was adopted by the old Congress, even as the Constitution was being drafted. Professor Bradford plays upon our present familiarity with many of these things, to inform us that "the Declaration of Independence is not very revolutionary at all. Nor the Revolution itself. Nor the Constitution." But this is to read history backwards, to pretend that the man was never a child, or that something was never new because it is not longer so!

I have observed many times that the independence of the United States was accomplished by a Declaration that constituted a political act without parallel in the history of the world. Professor Bradford opposes this thesis in writing that

> only a relativist or historicist could argue that American conservatism should be an utterly unique phenomenon, without antecedents which predate 1776, and unconnected with the mainstream of English and European thought and practice known to our forefathers in colonial times.[6]

But I never said or implied that the principles of the American Revolution were "without antecedents." No one would insist more than I that the colonies had enjoyed a learning process, of nearly two centuries, in constitutionalism and the rule of law. Some of the ideas incorporated into the Declaration—including the connection between equality and justice—had a history of more than two thousand years. But the rooting of constitutionalism, and the rule of law in a doctrine of universal human rights, in the political act of a people declaring independence, *is* unique and unprecedented.[7] Professor Bradford denies that the Declaration is revolutionary—or that it is unique—because he denies that it contains a declaration of universal human rights. And, I admit, if there were no such declaration, then the Declaration would cease to be everything I have claimed for it. Our debate turns upon what it is we find in the famous second paragraph. Professor Bradford, like Willmoore Kendall—and indeed like Chief Justice Taney in the case of Dred Scott—expends a great deal of ingenuity in pretending that the words do not mean what they plainly do mean.

> We hold these truths to be self-evident, that all men are created equal, that they are endowed by their Creator with certain unalienable rights, that among these are life, liberty, and the pursuit of happiness.

Because of the rights here affirmed—but only because of them—the American people are said to have a right to resist any attempt "to reduce them under absolute despotism." Professor Bradford thinks that white Americans had the right to resist despotism, because somehow such a right had become prescriptive under British tradition. Leaving aside the question of how such a tradition could have originated, we merely insist that that is not what the Declaration says. It says that *all* men have a right to resist despotism, and because all Americans are men, all Americans have this right. The right to resist despotism, that is, the right *not* to be slaves, is possessed equally by every human being on the face of the earth. That some might not have the capacity to make good this right, lacking either the power or the inclination, is nothing to the purpose. The form of the proposition contained in the second paragraph implies by unbreakable necessity, that unless the rights mentioned are possessed by everyone, they are possessed by no one. That is what the Signers said, and that, I am convinced, is what they meant.

The proposition that all men are created equal is, on the most elementary level, a principle of political obligation. It occurs in a context in which men are withdrawing their allegiance from an authority that has lost its legitimacy, and are transferring that allegiance to a new repository of legitimate authority. It is a principle for distinguishing when it is that men are, and when they are not, under a duty to obey. For anyone to argue, as does Professor Bradford, that the Signers of the Declaration did not understand their principles to apply to all men—in particular that they did not apply to Negro slaves—it would be necessary for him to find evidence that they (or anyone of the Revolutionary generation who had deliberately subscribed to the principles of the Declaration) considered that slaves had a *duty* to obey. That slaves may have been under a *necessity* to obey—or that the Signers or anyone else considered it expedient to place them under such a necessity—is nothing to the purpose. Abraham Lincoln, and many others, argued that in some sense American slavery was a necessity, imposed by circumstances, on both masters and slaves. Whether or not such an argument was disingenuous we need not enter into here. What is relevant is that such an argument in no way contradicts the opinion that the rights set forth in the second paragraph of the Declaration are universal rights. To say that white men have such rights, but that black men did not, would indeed have been inconsistent with the language of the Declaration. Professor Bradford is on common ground with the Marxist and Black Power historians of recent years, who have all along maintained that the Declaration was a bourgeois or racist document, never intended to be understood in the universalistic sense in which it is expressed. None of them has produced any such evidence of inconsistency as I have demanded, nor have they tried to show why any other evidence ought to be acceptable. I shall look forward to seeing whether Professor Bradford can supply this defect in his brief.

Professor Bradford's polemic against what he is pleased to call "the heresy of equality" occurs on at least two levels. On the one hand, he denies that there is any politically relevant sense in which it can be said with any truth that all men are created equal. On the other hand, he denies that the Signers of the Declaration meant it in any of the politically relevant senses attributed to it by Jefferson or the arch-heretic, Abraham Lincoln. Professor Bradford launches his attack by denying that there is any difference between what I had called the Old Liberalism—which demands equality of opportunity (which Professor Bradford correctly identifies with equality of rights)—and the New Liberalism, which demands equality of results. "Contrary to most Liberals, new and old," he writes,

> . . . it is nothing less than sophistry to distinguish between equality of opportunity (equal starts in the "race of life") and equality of condition (equal results). For only those who *are* equal can take equal advantage of a given circumstance. And there is no man equal to any other, except perhaps in the special and politically untranslatable, understanding of the Deity, *Not intellectually or physically or economically or even morally. Not equal!* Such is, of course, the genuinely self-evident proposition [Emphasis by Bradford].[8]

We have already seen that Professor Bradford maintains that neither the Declaration, the Revolution itself, or the Constitution are ("contrary to Professor Jaffa") very revolutionary. They became revolutionary, he says, "Only [because of] Mr. Lincoln and those who gave him support, both in his day and in the following century."[9] This is Bradford's expression of Kendall's thesis, that Abraham Lincoln had somehow "derailed" an American political tradition that had not heretofore worshipped the golden calf of equality. Yet Bradford, like Kendall, is doing little more than paraphrase Senator John C. Calhoun, in his great speech on the Oregon Bill, in the Senate, June 27, 1848. All the essentials are there, only with this difference: the arch-heretic is Jefferson instead of Lincoln!

In his speech, Calhoun calls "the most false and dangerous of all political errors" a proposition which, he said, "had become an axiom in the minds of a vast many on both sides of the Atlantic," a proposition which is "repeated daily from tongue to tongue, as an established and incontrovertible truth."[10] This is the proposition that "all men are born free and equal," a proposition which occurs in this precise form, not in the Declaration of Independence, but in the Massachusetts Bill of Rights (1780). But the doctrine it embodies was endemic to political public opinion in the revolutionary generation, as I have demonstrated by citing its variant expressions in seven of the original state constitutions, in "Equality as a Conservative Principle."

Calhoun refutes this dangerous falsehood by declaring that men are not born, that on the contrary only infants are born! And infants are so far from being either free or equal, that they are in a condition of perfectly unfree dependence.[11] He then takes up the proposition in the Declaration of Independence, that "all men are created equal." This form of expression, he says, "though less dangerous, is not less erroneous." Calhoun does not explain why it is less dangerous, but we may suppose that to call all men by nature free, is more directly subversive of slavery than to call them equal. Calhoun then continues as follows:

> All men are not created. According to the Bible, only two—a man and a woman—ever were—and of these one was pronounced subordinate to the other. All others have come into the world by being born, and in no sense, as I have shown, either free or equal.[12]

Now Calhoun knew that he was here merely taking words in their wrong sense. He knew that when Jefferson had penned his immortal lines—for the universal approval of his patriot fellow-citizens—he was making assertions, not about particular individuals in any particular state of individual or social development, but about the entire human race, seen in the light of the Creation. He was distinguishing man, as man had been distinguished in philosophic discourse even before Socrates, from the beast on the one hand, and from God or the gods on the other. Indeed, he was distinguishing man, as man had been distinguished in the first chapter of *Genesis*, when God gave him dominion over all the brute creation, while subject to Himself. Jefferson was laying down a premise by which despotic rule might in certain cases be regarded as natural and legitimate: the case of man ruling beast, or God ruling man. But by this same premise it was seen that man does not differ from man, as man differs from beast, or as man differs from God. As Jefferson rephrased the same thought fifty years later, shortly before his death, some men are not born with saddles on their backs, and others, booted and spurred, to ride them! Legitimate government does not then arise directly from nature; and therefore it does arise from consent. As the citizens of Malden, Massachusetts declared, in their instructions to their representatives in the Continental Congress, May 27, 1776, "we can never be willingly subject to any other King than he who, being possessed of infinite wisdom, goodness, and rectitude, is alone fit to possess unlimited power."[13] It is in this eminently reasonable sense that the proposition that all men are created equal is to be understood. And so it was understood, until the serpent of slavery, tempted some Americans to understand it differently.

Professor Bradford has declared with strident emphasis, that no man is equal to any other, intellectually, physically, or morally. In his speech on the Dred Scott decision,[14] Abraham Lincoln also asserted that the Signers of Declaration did not intend to say that men were equal in color, size, intellect, moral development, or social capacity. And where Professor Bradford agrees with Abraham Lincoln we have, I suspect, a good practical definition of self-evident truth. But why cannot Professor Bradford understand that equality of *rights* is perfectly consistent with inequality of ability? Indeed, why cannot he understand that equality of rights is the *only* ground upon which inequality of ability can properly manifest itself?

Let us consider again the case of an exchange of shoes for grain. Should such an exchange be governed by the relative I.Q.'s, or moral reputation, or color, or the physical strength, of the buyer and the seller? Or should it be governed by the equal money value of the shoes and the grain? At bottom, an exchange of shoes for grain is an exchange between a shoemaker and a grain-grower. But what qualities of the shoemaker and the grain-grower are relevant to a just exchange, except those manifest in the shoes and the grain? Now good shoes should bring more money—and hence more grain—than poorly made shoes. But the good shoemaker can be known only by his shoes. To return less to the shoemaker for his labor, not because of the quality of the shoes, but because he is black (or, for that matter, because she is female), is manifestly unequal and hence unjust.

Professor Bradford has made the extraordinary assertion, that it is sophistry to distinguish equality of opportunity from equality of results. He observes that "only those who *are* equal can take equal advantage of a given circumstance." I confess myself unable to assign any intelligible meaning to this assertion. Does he mean that a fair start in a race is advantageous only to someone who is fast enough to win it? But this is nonsense. The purpose of the race is to find out who *is* the fastest, and this can be done only if the start of the race is fair. I think it useful here to distinguish an open race from a handicap race. Only an open race is a true race—that is, only a race in which every runner has a chance to compete, can reveal who it is who can run the fastest. And a true race is one in which everyone starts from the same line at the same time, and runs the same distance. Moreover, it is one in which none of the runners are hobbled, and none are given packs to carry. Or, alternatively, if hobbles or packs are part of the race, then everyone must be hobbled or burdened in exactly the same way. But it is precisely when everyone starts together in a fair race, that they do *not* end together. According to Professor Bradford, the "hue and cry over equality of opportunity and equal rights leads, *a fortiori*, to a final demand for equality of condition." But is it not evident; indeed, is it not *self-evident*, that the truth is the exact opposite? In a fair race, the natural inequalities of the runners emerge in the results, and these inequalities are expressed in the order of the finish. The only equality which we see—or wish to see—in the result, is the proportional equality of unequal prizes for unequal finishers.

Now what is a handicap race? A handicap race is one designed to overcome the natural inequality of the runners. It is one designed to give the slower runner an *equal* chance with the fastest runner. The handicapper does this by assigning a longer distance (or a later start) to the fast runner, and a shorter distance (or an earlier start) to the slow runner, and in theory, a perfectly handicapped race would be one in which everyone finished together. In practice, a perfectly handicapped race introduces the greatest amount of uncertainty into the outcome. Both theoretically and practically, handicapping overcomes natural ability in favor of equality of results. But Professor Bradford's prescriptive rights, in particular the prescriptive right of a master to own slaves, as against the equal natural rights he opposes, bring about a handicapped society. That they do produce a spurious "equality of results," is the testimony of the supreme spokesman for the old South.

In Calhoun's Oregon speech, speaking in defense of that social order which, Professor Bradford would have us believe, was a partnership in every virtue and all perfection, the Senator declared that

> With us [of the South] the two great divisions of society are not the rich and poor, but white and black; and all the former, the poor as well as the rich, belong to the upper class, and are respected and treated as equals, if honest and industrious; and hence have a position and pride of character of which neither poverty nor misfortune can deprive them.[15]

What a confession of moral blindness is this! All whites are assigned upper class status (if honest and industrious!), with pride of position and character assigned to them, without regard to their inequality of achievement or excellence. And all blacks are assigned lower class status (however honest or industrious) simply because they are black (free blacks not being distinguished from slaves.) All distinctions of virtue or intelligence are, in the decisive respect, assimilated to the single distinction of color. All intrinsically important human qualities are debased and degraded from the honors due to them, by the distinction of color alone. And except for the *inequality* resulting from color, the antebellum South, according to its most distinguished spokesman, produced the most perfect *equality of results*, in the race of life, that the world has ever seen!

Professor Bradford's case against the "heresy of equality," rests upon both logical and historical grounds. That is, he regards it both as false in itself, and false as a doctrine ascribed to the Founding Fathers. He denies that the doctrine of equal human rights can properly be found in the Declaration of Independence. To find it there is, he maintains, to misread the Declaration. Professor Bradford's argument is a theme with many variations, and it is sometimes difficult to detect the theme within the variation. But his case as a historical scholar—as distinct from a political philosopher—comes down to this. When the Declaration reads "all men are created equal," we are not to understand "men" to refer to *individual* human beings, but only to human beings in their *collective* capacity, acting politically within civil society as members of a "people."

> We are now prepared to ask [writes Professor Bradford] what Mr. Jefferson

and his sensible friends meant by "all men" and "created equal." Meant to-gether—*as a group*. . . .[16]

Professor Bradford, be it noted, thought Jefferson's *friends* were sensible. What they meant *as a group* (the emphasis is Bradford's) must be sensible, because of the friends. Jefferson's well-known strictures against slavery make it impossible for Professor Bradford ever to regard him as a sensible *individual*. However, one can only wonder why those sensible friends were so agreeable to having the non-sensible Jefferson draft the Declaration in the first place.

> The *exordium* of the Declaration begins . . . with an argument from history and with a definition of the voice addressing "the powers of the earth!" It is a "people," a "we" that are estranged from another "we." The peroration reads the same: "we," the "free and independent states," are united in our will to separation. . . . No contemporary liberal, new or old, can make use of that framework or take the customary liberties with what is contained by the construction. Nor coming to it by the path I have marked, may they, in honesty, see in "created equal" what they devoutly wish to find. "We," in that second sentence, signifies the colonials as the citizenry of the distinct colonies, not as individuals, but rather in their corporate capacity. There-fore, the following "all men"—created equal in their right to expect from any government to which they might submit freedom from corporate bondage . . . [hence] equal as one free state is as free as another. Nothing is maintained concerning the abilities or situations of individual persons. . . .[17]

We have quoted at length here, because we wished there to be no doubt that any assertions we make concerning Professor Bradford's text, are solidly grounded in that text. We observe, first of all, that Professor Bradford and I do not differ at all, concerning the proposi-tion that when the Signers of the Declaration speak of "one people" or "we" or "these united colonies," they were referring to them-selves, and those whom they represented, in a corporate or collec-tive, or political capacity. Indeed, I suspect that I go further than Professor Bradford, since I am convinced that "one people" meant just that, and that the several "peoples" of the several colonies or states, were already formed into one single people. And I hold—with Presidents Jackson and Lincoln—that the several states also were formed into one indissoluble union. But how in the world can the expression "men" be synonymous with "people"? Consider the text: "We hold these truths to be self-evident, that all men are created equal, that they are endowed by their Creator with certain unalienable rights. . . ." The first "We" is indeed the colonials, or the former colonials, citizens of the formerly distinct (but now united) colonies. But why are "we" endowed with "certain unalienable rights?" According to Professor Bradford, it is because they possessed those rights as colonials. But why should they possess those rights when they are no longer colonials? Rights granted by civil society are rights which can be taken away by civil society. But the Declaration here is most explicit. The rights of which it speaks are not civil or political rights, rights resulting from human or positive law. They are rights with which they had been "endowed by their Creator." Unless therefore Professor Bradford believes that the Creator endowed colonial Americans with rights with which he had not endowed other human beings, then the "men" in the phrase "all men are created equal" *must* be a more comprehensive category than the men in the "we" who hold these truths.

It is also a rule of interpretation for archaic documents that the meaning of words or phrases is to be sought in the light of contemporary usage. In Calhoun's Oregon speech, he assumed as a matter of course that "all men are born free and equal," and "all men are created equal" were mere variations of expression for the same fundamental idea. The former was, as we have noted, taken from the Massachusetts Bill of Rights. Article I of that document reads in full as follows.

> All men are born free and equal, and have certain natural, essential, and inalienable rights; among which may be reckoned the right of enjoying and defending their lives and liberties; that of acquiring, possessing, and protecting property; in fine, that of seeking and obtaining their safety and happiness.[18]

Can anyone doubt that the "men" referred to here are *individuals*, not societies of men in any collective sense? Instead of being "endowed by their Creator" with certain rights, they are born with them. And the rights with which they are born, are said to be "natural, essential, and unalienable," the three terms clearly being synonymous. But Professor Bradford's reading, as we have seen, regards the rights which the collective "we" declares, to be rights held only "in their corporate capacity." Such rights are ineluctably civil or political, they could not possibly be called "natural" or "essential," any more than they could be called "unalienable."

But we may, I think, settle the matter beyond cavil. In the very Preamble of the Massachusetts Bill of Rights, we find the following:

> The body politic is formed by a voluntary association of individuals; it is a social compact by which the whole people covenants with each citizen and each citizen with the whole people that all shall be governed by certain laws for the common good.[19]

Since the Massachusetts Bill of Rights was adopted in 1780, I submit further these lines from the Virginia Bill of Rights, adopted less than a month before the Declaration of Independence.

> That all men are by nature equally free and independent, and have certain inherent rights [inherent being synonymous with natural, essential, and unalienable], of which when they enter into a state of society, they cannot by any compact deprive or divest their posterity. . . .[20]

Can there then be any reasonable doubt, can there indeed be any possible doubt, that for the revolutionary generation, human beings, as human beings, as men, had rights antecedent to, and independent of, civil society? Or that civil society, properly so called (that is, legitimate civil society), resulted from an agreement among men possessed of such rights? Can there then be any doubt that when the Declaration speaks of "all men" being created equal, it does indeed then refer to individuals?

This record is not, contrary to Professor Bradford, an invention of liberals, new or old. Had John C. Calhoun, when he delivered his Oregon speech in 1848, had the slightest suspicion that this interpretation of the Declaration was a perversity of abolitionist propaganda, he would certainly have been as forward as Professor Bradford in pointing it out. Yet in the peroration of that speech he declared that

> We now begin to experience the danger of admitting so great an error to have a place in the declaration of our independence. . . . It had strong hold on the mind of Mr. Jefferson, the author of that document [Calhoun did not see the difference between Jefferson and his sensible friends], which caused him to take an utterly false view of the subordinate relation of the black to the white race in the South; and to hold in consequence, that the latter, though utterly

unqualified to possess liberty, were as fully entitled to both liberty and equality as the former; and that to deprive them of it was unjust and immoral.[21]

Clearly, it never occurred for a moment to Calhoun that the "men" in "all men are created equal" did not refer to Negroes, however erroneous he may have believed the proposition to have been. We see then that the American Civil War resulted from a new revolution, a revolution in opinion in the South. That revolution denied the axiomatic premise of the older, better Revolution, which had declared—and meant—that all men are created equal.

Professor Bradford has a great many things to say about Abraham Lincoln, none of them complimentary. His remarks cover a spectrum that ranges all the way from the nonsensical to the absurd. As a specimen, we cite one which even he felt constrained to put into the small print of the end notes. After observing a comparison of Lincoln to Bismarck and Lenin by Edmund Wilson, he adds:

> Another useful analogue (a firm higher law man, and no legalist or historicist) is Adolf Hitler. For he writes in *Mein Kampf* that "human rights break state rights," calls for illegal as well as legal instruments in "wars of rebellion against enslavement within and without," observes that all governments by oppression plead the law, and concludes, "I believe that I am acting in the sense of the Almighty Creator . . . fighting for the Lord's work."[22]

I think that if Professor Bradford had searched long enough he might have found a documented quotation from Hitler, in which he had said that some of his best friends were Jews. Such a quotation would have had exactly the same significance as the one presented above.

Professor Bradford does not like Lincoln's attachment to higher law doctrine. In particular, he does not like the fusion, in Lincoln's rhetoric, of higher law drawn from both the natural law, as expressed in the Declaration of Independence, and from the divine law, as found in the Bible. Let us concede that Lincoln was the greatest master of this rhetorical fusion. But it is utterly misleading to suppose that it was his invention, or that it was more characteristic of him than of any one of a large number of his contemporaries, North or South.

According to Professor Bradford, the House Divided speech—

with which Lincoln opened the campaign for Douglas' Senate seat in 1858—"was, beyond any question, a Puritan declaration of war." It was so, says Bradford, because, quoting the words of Lincoln's "one-time friend, Alexander Stephens," it "put the institution of nearly one-half the states under the ban of public opinion and national condemnation.'" Bradford continues:

> Of course the central motif of the House Divided speech . . . echoes the Bible (Mark 3:25): Christ speaking of the undivided hosts of Satan. Lincoln's authority is thus, by association, elevated to the level of the hieratic. But he added something to that mixture. The myth that slavery will either be set on its way to extinction . . . or else all states will eventually become slave states establishes a false dilemma. . . . Thus he participates in what Richard Hofstadter calls the "paranoid style" in politics.[23]

Later on, Bradford adds, in words which he italicized for emphasis:

> *For houses are always divided, in some fashion or another.*[24]

Thus Lincoln, invoking the higher law, natural and divine, against slavery, demanding that the house be undivided, was introducing a revolutionary, gnostic, antinomian morality, as the ground of politics. He was thus assuring that politics would forever after be a crusade against sin, the sin to be defined, not by priests, but by egalitarian, ideological politicians.

Since Bradford has introduced Alexander Stephens as a witness against Lincoln, it would be particularly instructive to see how Stephens' views of the crisis of the divided house compared with Lincoln's. In December, 1860, shortly after South Carolina had adopted its Ordinance of Secession, Lincoln wrote to Stephens, saying that

> you think slavery is *right*, and should be extended, and we think it is *wrong*, and should be restricted. That, I suppose, is the rub. It certainly is the only substantial difference between us."[25]

Stephens, it should be remarked, was a Southern moderate. As an old Whig, he was a strong Unionist, and fought against secession in his state of Georgia as long as he could. But he went with his state when it left the Union, and became Vice President of the Confederate States of America. After the adoption of the Confederate Constitution, he propounded a defense of the new regime, which has come down in history as the "Corner Stone" speech. It has its name from precisely the same source as Lincoln's House Divided speech. Both are built around biblical texts. Stephens certainly elevates his doctrine to the level of the hieratic, as Bradford puts it, every bit as much as Lincoln. But Stephens' speech is more than a defense of the new regime. It is the most comprehensive Southern reply to *all* of Lincoln's speeches, from 1854 to 1860, of any that the record of the times shows. What the speech proves, beyond doubt, is that Lincoln was perfectly accurate when he said that Stephens' thinking slavery right, and Lincoln's thinking it wrong, was the *only* substantial difference between them. In every other respect, as we shall see, Stephens was in *agreement* with Lincoln, and in *disagreement* with Professor Bradford.

Lincoln held, in virtually all his speeches between 1854 and 1860—notably in the debates with Douglas, and in the Cooper Union speech—that the Founding Fathers had all regarded slavery as a great moral wrong. They had inherited slavery as part of their colonial legacy, and its presence among them imposed certain "necessities" which they were powerless to change. But they supposed that slavery was nonetheless "in course of ultimate extinction," and although they gave guarantees to slavery while it should last, they did not expect it to last. Its presence was tolerable because, but only because, they expected it gradually to die out. The House was not a Divided House, in Lincoln's sense, if the moral wrong of slavery were acknowledged, and public policy based upon that acknowledgement as a premise. What does Alexander Stephens say about this?

> The prevailing ideas entertained by [Jefferson] and most of the leading statesmen at the time of the formation of the old Constitution, were that the enslavement of the African was in violation of the laws of nature: that it was wrong in principle, socially, morally, and politically. It was an evil they knew not well how to deal with, but the general opinion of the men of that day was, that somehow or other, in the order of Providence, the institution would be evanescent and pass away.[26]

We see now that Jefferson's sensible friends were no more sensible than he! It is axiomatic for Stephens that "most of the leading statesmen" of the time, were antislavery. All of them understood "all men are created equal" to include *all* men, and therefore to include Negroes. It was the "general opinion of the men of that day" that slavery was a transient phenomenon. Hence general opinion agreed with Lincoln that at the Founding slavery was in course of ultimate extinction, and that the House of the Founders was not a Divided House.

Stephens does not disagree by one iota with Lincoln's interpretation of the Founding. *But he disagrees with the Founding.* "Those ideas," he writes, viz., of the Founding Fathers,

> were fundamentally wrong. They rested upon the assumption of the equality of the races. This was an error. It was a sandy foundation, and the idea of a government built upon it; when the "storm came and the wind blew, it fell."[27]

The quotation by Stephens is taken from Mark, 7:26, 27. Jesus is speaking, and says, "And every one who hears these words of mine and does not do them will be like a foolish man who built his house upon sand: and the rain fell, and the floods came, and the winds blew and beat against the house, and it fell; and great was the fall of it." What was the sandy foundation? It was the doctrine that the races were equal. And what is rock which, asserts Stephens, is the truth upon which a government can stand? What is it for which he claims, by analogy, the hieratic authority of Jesus himself?

> Our new government [declared Stephens] is founded upon exactly the opposite idea; its foundations are laid, its corner stone rests upon the great truth that the negro is not the equal to the white man. That slavery—the subordination to the superior race, is his natural and normal condition.
> This our new Government [the Confederate States of America] is the first in the history of the world, based upon this great physical and moral truth. This truth has been slow in the process of its development, like all other truths in the various departments of science. . . .[28]

We have seen Professor Bradford's distaste for political novelty. Time and again, he has defended the cause of the Confederacy as the cause of traditional society attempting to preserve tradition against a radical break with the past, a break enforced by Lincoln's militant, uniformitarian Unionism. But here we find a most eminent apologist for the Confederacy, its supremely articulate Vice President, in March, 1861, declaring the cause of the Confederacy to be the *exact opposite* of what Professor Bradford has declared it to be.

Not only does Stephens say that the Confederacy is the first government of its kind in the history of the world, but he says that it is based upon a truth that has emerged from the progress of science. Although he says that such truths are slow in their process of development, it is also the case that they cause profound upheavals where they make their appearance. The examples which Stephens himself gives span less than two centuries. The fault of the Founding Fathers was not that they were perverse, but that the progress of science had not enlightened them. Stephens' doctrine is then not merely a commitment to novelty, but a commitment to a perpetual revolution of morals and politics, whenever the progress of science shall reveal new truths. It is the most radical denial possible, of that "funded wisdom of the ages" in which Professor Bradford would have us place our faith. It is a denial of such permanent standards as are incorporated in the natural law teaching of the Declaration of Independence.

Stephens compares the new truth about the races, to the discoveries of Galileo, Adam Smith, and Harvey. Harvey's theory of the circulation of the blood, he says, was not admitted by "a single one of the medical profession living at the time," yet now it is "universally acknowledged." "May we not," asks Stephens, "therefore

> look forward with confidence to the ultimate universal acknowledgment of the truths upon which our system rests? It is the first government ever instituted upon principles of strict conformity to nature, and the ordination of Providence, in furnishing the materials of human society. Many governments have been founded upon the principle of certain classes; but the classes thus enslaved, were of the same race, and in violation of the laws of nature. Our system commits no such violation of nature's laws. The negro, by nature, or by the curse of Canaan, is fitted for that condition which he occupies in our system.[29]

Surely, Abraham Lincoln never set forth the case for an undivided house with greater assurance or conviction! Nor did Lincoln appeal to greater authority, either natural or divine, in support of his version of what the undivided house should be. Yet there is something self-contradictory in Stephens' appeal, as there is not in Lincoln's. Why should it have come to be known only so recently, that the Negro is fitted by nature only for slavery? Especially if the "cause" of that nature is the curse of Canaan? Whence could it have arisen, that so enlightened a generation as that of the Founding Fathers should have been so completely wrong about so fundamental a reality? For it is clear that Stephens *does* regard them as enlightened, in all respects except one. The many governments which, he says, were founded upon "the principles of certain classes," is certainly meant to encompass all the unequal regimes of the old world. The founding that began on July 4, 1776, is certainly, albeit indirectly, endorsed by Stephens, in precisely the sense in which we have endorsed it. It too must have been "the first in the history of the world," in just the way in which we have described it above. Stephens has no quarrel—any more than did Calhoun— with a system which is radically egalitarian as far as white men are concerned. But, like Calhoun, he thinks that this egalitarianism can only be properly realized, upon the foundation of Negro slavery. From Stephens' perspective the Revolution accomplished by the Declaration and the Constitution, was perfect in its kind. There is no question but that that Revolution represented a break with everything that went before it. But it needed one further step forward in enlightenment—the step represented by the discovery of the inferiority of the Negro race. (Never mind if this opinion is inconsistent with the idea of unknowable future scientific progress.)

> The architect, in the construction of buildings, lays the foundation with proper materials. . . . The substratum of our society is made of the material fitted by nature for it, and by experience we know that it is best, not only for the superior, but for the inferior race that it should be so. It is indeed in conformity with the ordinance of the Creator. . . . The great objects of humanity are best attained when conformed to His laws and decrees, in the formation of government, as well as in all things else. Our Confederacy is founded upon principles in strict conformity with these laws. This stone which was first rejected by the first builders "is become the chief stone of the corner" in our new edifice.[30]

Thus ends the first and greatest apology for the Confederacy, made in the flush of its confidence in long life and prosperity. Stephens'

159

apology *after* the Civil War, contained in his *Constitutional View of the War Between the States*, is very different. The "cornerstone" sinks from sight, and States' rights, as the ground of constitutionalism, replaces it. But I think the Corner Stone speech is the more authentic, as revealing the character of the Confederacy when it felt full confidence in its principles. The "corner stone" quotation comes from Psalms, 118:22. "The stone which the builders refused is become the head stone of the corner." It appears however in both Matthew and Mark, where Jesus quotes it, and quotes it in such a way as to indicate that he, or his teaching, is the stone in question. Certainly Stephens yielded nothing to Lincoln, in his assumption of what Bradford calls "hieratic" authority.

We began this part of our essay by giving Professor Bradford's quotation from Adolf Hitler, in which he shows that Hitler, like Lincoln, was a "firm higher law man." Hitler, we saw, like Lincoln believed that "human rights" take precedence of "state rights"; and that Hitler, like Lincoln believed he was "fighting for the Lord's work." But we see now that Union and Confederate causes did not differ, with respect to being higher law causes. Had Hitler looked back for precedent, it is not likely that he would have looked to Abraham Lincoln. All the precedent he would have needed in the higher law sense was certainly present in Stephens' Corner Stone speech. And in the decisive sense, that speech, like the cause it represented, would have been entirely congenial. Certainly Hitler's doctrines of racial inequality went much beyond that of Stephens. Yet when Hitler spoke of "human rights," he certainly did not do so in the sense of Lincoln or Jefferson. "Human rights" were for him, primarily and essentially the rights of the master race. And the Confederate States of America represented the first time in human history, that a doctrine of a master race was fully and systematically set forth as the ground of a regime. More precisely, it was the first time that such a doctrine was set forth *on the authority of modern science*. It was this authority that made it so persuasive, and so pernicious.

National Socialism and Marxist Communism are, as I have argued elsewhere,[31] alternative versions of the social Darwinism that was so rife in nineteenth century thought. They are alternative foundations of the totalitarian tyrannies that have so blotted and befouled the life of man in our time. That at least one of them never took root in the United States we owe, more than to any other man, to Abraham Lincoln. Let us carry on his work, building upon that rock upon which he built his undivided house, the teaching that, with respect to the rights to life, liberty, and the pursuit of happiness, "*all* men are created equal."

Appendix

Political Philosophy and Honor:
The Leo Strauss Dissertation Award

> In what way shall we bury you? How ever you wish, if you
> can catch me, and I do not escape from you. Then he laughed
> gently, and turned and looked at us, and said: I do not, men,
> persuade Crito, that I am that Socrates who has been dis-
> cussing, and conducting the argument; but he thinks I am
> that other one, whom he will see a little later as a dead body,
> and asks, how he will bury me.
>
> —*Phaedo, 115 C*

NOTHING perhaps better illustrates the enduring character of political philosophy than the enduring presence of its body servants,
whose piety would inter the soul of the teaching with the body of the
teacher.

As its annual meeting in 1974 the American Political Science
Association established the Leo Strauss Annual Dissertation Award
in political philosophy. This action followed a petition addressed to
the Council of the Association, signed by some forty–four distinguished teachers and scholars. Of these, it appeared, more than half
were former students of Leo Strauss. The petition declared, among
other things, that:

> There is at present no such award in the field of political philosophy. We
> believe the establishment of one to be peculiarly important and timely. It is
> important that the Association signalize to the profession in general, and to
> graduate students in this field, its recognition of political philosophy as one of
> the important traditions within the discipline.

In 1959 Leo Strauss published a book with the title essay, "What Is
Political Philosophy?" In that essay, Strauss wrote that:

> Today, political philosophy is in a state of decay and perhaps of putrefaction, if
> it has not vanished altogether. Not only is there complete disagreement

162

regarding its subject matter, its methods, and its function; its very possibility in any form has become questionable.

Familiar as I was with this and many similar passages in Strauss' writings, I was compelled to wonder at this "important and timely . . . recognition of political philosophy." Had the corpse suddenly sprung to life since 1959? Or had Strauss been utterly wrong then (and indeed to the last moment of his life) concerning the state of political philosophy? Certainly the latter seemed more likely than the former. But if so, so much the more inappropriate such an award to honor a man who was so mistaken. In any event, the logical disjunction seemed to me to be complete, between Strauss' assertion of "complete disagreement" concerning what political philosophy was, and an award by those in complete disagreement, in honor of Leo Strauss.

On February 4, 1975 I addressed the following letter to the editor of *The American Political Science Review*. Needless to say, it was refused publication both in the *Review*, and its sister journal, *PS*:

"When I arrived in Chicago for the meeting of the A.P.S.A. last August, I learned—after the fact—of the establishment of a Leo Strauss Annual Dissertation Award. At the time, I was too surprised to react in any way other than by astonishment. Since then I have given it much thought, and the more I have thought of it, the less I have liked it.

"In my own eulogy of Strauss, I observed with no little diffidence that to honor a man implies competence in the one honoring, no less than excellence in him who is honored. To doubt the former necessarily involves doubting the latter as well. While there is no escape from this dilemma, one may nevertheless approach it with a certain prudence. This I fear the promoters of the Award have not done. . . .

"Leo Strauss was at odds with the main-stream—or perhaps one should say the various mainstreams—of the political science profession throughout his career. His best known statement about the majority of his colleagues concluded by declaring that, like Nero, they were fiddling while Rome burned. They were saved from the reproach of being Neronian, he said, only by the fact that they did not know they were fiddling, and that they did not know that Rome was burning.

"Strauss' contempt was warmly reciprocated within the profession. This was shown by the attack, not only on Strauss, but on his school, by Schaar and Wolin, in the pages of the *A.P.S.R.*, in an extended review (followed by rebuttals and replies) of *Essays on the Scientific Study of Politics*. This volume, by Strauss' former students, concluded with his famous Epilogue. On the whole, Strauss enjoyed this adversary relationship. *Solet Aristoteles quaerere pugnam* was the epigraph for his Walgreen Lectures in 1949. And Aristotle himself did not join battle more assiduously than Leo Strauss. How then is an Association consisting overwhelmingly of those whom Strauss attacked, and who attacked him, during his life, to agree on the standards of excellence to be honored in his name?

"The motion in favor of the Strauss Award speaks of 'the universal recognition of Strauss' exemplary devotion to the philosophic study of politics.' In truth, however, there has been no such recognition of Strauss, nor did he ever wish for it. If there can be no universal recognition of the philosophic study of politics, how can there be universal recognition of Strauss' devotion to it? If Strauss ever taught anything, it is the impossibility, not to mention the undesirability, of such universal opinions. Indeed, he was particularly averse to any alleged universal opinion in favor of a philosophic study of politics. Could there be such an opinion, he thought, it might lead to the establishment of the universal tyranny of the universal homogenous state. That was his contention in his debate with Kojeve in *On Tyranny*.

"The proposal to honor Strauss with an annual dissertation award bears a resemblance to a similar proposal made by the first political scientist, Hippodamus, as reported in the second book of the *Politics*. How will the field of 'political philosophy' be defined for purposes of the award? The profession generally speaks of 'political theory.' And political theory is usually divided into 'normative' and 'empirical.' But this latter distinction is founded on that between 'facts' and 'values,' a distinction that Strauss attacked again and again. I cannot imagine anyone, familiar with Strauss' work, who would impute validity to the distinction between normative and empirical theory. Yet most dissertations in "theory" will probably be based upon it. Will they be eligible for the award or not?

"The distinction between the 'normative' and the 'empirical' is paralleled by certain others, e.g., that between theory and practice. Is the field of 'political philosophy' to consist in the study of the books of those called political philosophers, or is it equally the philosophic study of political things, e.g., the words and deeds of politicians, legislators, judges, and generals, and including the study of constitutions, wars, elections, and trials. Although Strauss' own work consisted mainly in reading and interpreting philosophic books, the books he read—and praised—frequently encouraged a much more inclusive conception of the field of political philosophy. This was certainly true of Aristotle's *Politics*. But if the scope of the award is to be so broad how will the selection process deal with it?

"But this brings us to the central problem, that of the judges themselves. Are they to be so-called 'Straussians.' If they are, I can assure my professional colleagues that it will not be long before differences as acute as any others will show themselves in any group so denominated. But surely, it would be as foolish as it would be impracticable, to try to appoint judges with such a bias. The American Political Science Association is, within limits, and in a manner appropriate to a professional association, a constitutional democracy. A prize committee of the Association *ought* therefore to reflect and to represent the standards of a majority.

"And I think, it inevitably will do so. As we all know, constitutional majorities are themselves almost invariably coalitions of differing groups, who have agreed to disagree on some things, in order to act together on others. It is not difficult to anticipate how this process will affect an awards committee. There will be logrolling between factions, so that a work reflecting one persuasion will win one year, to be followed by one of another the next. In neither case, will the best work be chosen on its own merits. Any work that attempts to make peace among the factions by appealing to some common denominator among them, will succeed only by calculated mediocrity. Works of genuine brilliance and distinction will seldom if ever have a chance, because they will antagonize by their uncompromising superiority. It is virtually inconceivable that any of Strauss' books, had they been submitted as dissertations, could have won such an award. The prize will, therefore, discourage, rather than encourage the emulation of Leo Strauss. I should add that among the minor features that I find objectionable, is making an *annual* award, without regard to whether there is, in any year, a dissertation of sufficient merit. Nor should there, I think, ever be such an award, without an assurance of publication. Not only is publication a much better incentive than money, but it allows the work of the prize committee, as well as that of the prize winner, to be judged by a more impartial public.

"Leo Strauss was not a political man. He sought wisdom rather than honor. He certainly wanted recognition, in part to reassure himself in the critical and skeptical attitude he maintained even towards his own work. But he also felt that recognition of his work should form part of a learning process, that benefited the recognizers, and made them thereby more competent judges. Political honors are produced mainly by agreement; and, as Strauss taught, agreement leads to peace, but not to truth. The truth-seeker, on the contrary, is accustomed to seeking a fight. We honor Strauss best by carrying on the fight for truth, even if that may mean opposing so unwise an enterprise as an annual dissertation award in the name of Leo Strauss."

Copies of this letter were sent to many members of the profession, including most of those who had signed the petition for the award. Many I knew to be keen students of the problem of knowledge, so central to the problem of political knowledge, and hence to the question of what is political philosophy. They knew that I had asked, in effect, how one could offer a prize for the best drawing of a horse, to those who had never seen a horse. Or, alternatively, how a panel of judges could award a prize for a drawing of a horse, if the judges themselves had never seen a horse, or did not know that they had ever seen a horse. Suppose that one judge thought a horse very much like a bear, another that it was much more like a lion, while a third was convinced it closely resembled a camel, but that all would instantly agree that anyone who pointed to a real horse, must be an ass!

The response to my letter may be characterized on the whole as a sullen silence, punctuated by muttered imprecations. I received altogether three written replies. Only one respondent was candid in agreement, saying that he doubted anyone would ever receive the Strauss Award to whom Strauss himself would have given a grade higher than a "C." The others, while not venturing to contradict either my premises or my reasoning, rejected the conclusion. Of course, I did not need this exercise to persuade myself of the very limited possibilities of persuasion in such a case. It was thirty years since I had first sat at the feet of Leo Strauss, and heard him discourse upon Polemarchus' refusal to hear why it might be good for Socrates and Glaucon to return to Athens from Piraeus. Still, it was more than merely ironical that such a refusal should come from those who have undertaken to honor Leo Strauss, and to promote the good of political philosophy.

In the murmured discontent that sometimes broke the sullen silence, I detected the objection that my argument, although perhaps correct in "theory," was nonetheless wrong in "practice." I was familiar with Aristotle's conception of prudence (*phronesis*), in accordance with which political speeches—or documents belonging to the genus of political speech—may be considered not merely as words, but as deeds. Strauss often quoted Lord Macaulay's famous formulation, that "If they effect that which they are intended to effect, they are rational though they may be contradictory. If they fail of obtaining their end, they are absurd." But what end was the Leo Strauss Award intended to effect? Let us suppose it was the end announced by the promoters, *viz.*, the "recognition of political philosophy as one of the important traditions within the discipline." We need not further labor the point that one does not promote the recognition of something that one has not recognized, by pretending to recognize it. But we observe that the promoters call political philosophy "one of the important traditions *within* the discipline." Who that knows anything of Strauss' work, does not know of his relentless denial that political philosophy, properly so called, was *one* among *many*? To provide only one of many possible illustrations, we submit this passage from "What Is Political Philosophy?"

> The goal of the general is victory, whereas the goal of the statesman is the common good. What victory means is not essentially controversial, but the meaning of the common good is essentially controversial. The ambiguity of the political goal is due to its controversial character. Thus the temptation

arises to deny, or to evade the comprehensive character of politics and to treat politics as one compartment among many. But this temptation must be resisted if it is necessary to face our situation as human beings, i.e. the whole situation.

One of the least invidious things one can say of the Strauss Award is that it exhibits a kind of amnesia in regard to what Strauss himself had insisted was the necessary condition for the possibility of political philosophy. Perhaps it also reflected a weariness with the controversy that always surrounded Strauss. But that controversy did not arise from any idiosyncrasy of Leo Strauss; it was intrinsic to the nature of his vocation. If it seemed to be idiosyncratic, that stemmed from the fact that he took that vocation with greater seriousness than any other man of his time. The desire to make one's peace with the world is understandable. But it is the task of political philosophy to ask, what is that world with which one would make one's peace? To call that political philosophy, which asks that question in anything less than a perfectly comprehensive manner, is to abandon the possibility of a genuine answer. Yet upon the possibility of a genuine answer, rests the fate of everything that is—or ought to be—dear to us. Such at any rate was Strauss' conviction.

We also observe that the promoters of the Award—in the interest, no doubt, of professional harmony and democratic consensus—not only dethrone political philosophy from its monarchical estate, but describe it as a "tradition." Without demeaning or impugning the traditions, and the many traditional things, that are very dear to us, we must nonetheless ask, why in the world should political philosophy—a discipline of the mind—be commended as a "tradition?" Aristotle tells us that the remains of the ancient laws are "altogether foolish," and that what men seek is not the ancestral but the good [*Politics*, 1269 a 1–5]. Political philosophy comes to light with the discovery of the distinction between the ancestral (the old which is one's own), and the good. If there were but a single tradition in the world, such a discovery would not have taken place, and indeed would be unnecessary. But there are in fact many traditions of mankind, and they proclaim many contradictory things about the right way of life. If then political philosophy is itself nothing more than a tradition, it is utterly without power to guide us in the face of conflicting traditions. For that which is itself but one among many, cannot tell us what the whole—the one compounded of many—ought to be.

According to Strauss, "the character of classical political philosophy appears with the greatest clarity from Plato's *Laws,* which is his political work par excellence." The *Laws* is a dialogue between three old men which takes place on the island of Crete, by tradition the home of the oldest Greek laws. One's first impression, says Strauss, is that the Athenian, the principal interlocutor, has come to Crete to discover the best laws. But one soon discovers that on the contrary he has come "to introduce into Crete new laws and institutions, truly good laws and institutions." The Cretans, Strauss reminds us, were famous not only for their laws, but for their mendacity; and the two, it appears, are not unrelated. For the authority of their laws was derived from the assurance that they had been given by Minos, son of Zeus. Have not the promoters of the Strauss Award, ignoring the distinction between the one and the many, and between the traditional and the good, promoted something much less akin to Strauss' own Socratic rationalism, than to Cretan traditionalism?

Another correspondent had pronounced my letter to the editor of the *American Political Science Review* to be "overly sectarian." This objection—made without further explanation—struck me as having a peculiar irony. To be sectarian usually means to be unduly narrow. Yet I was defending political philosophy from a narrowing of its scope, and from its "domestication" within the "tradition" of current American political science. Still, the paradox of philosophy— the attempt to replace opinions of the whole, with knowledge of the whole—appearing as a sectarian cause, is as old as philosophy itself. Hence I took this objection with some seriousness, and responded as follows:

". . . I agree as far as the adjective which makes it impossible to agree to the adverb. Strauss himself was the Great Sectarian of our time, in much the same sense that Doctor Johnson meant when he said that the Devil was the First Whig. ['. . . philosophy, as distinct from wisdom, necessarily appears in the form of philosophic schools or sects.' Strauss, in *On Tyranny,* p. 208]

"Francis Bacon said of the Greek philosophy . . . that it was 'like the boyhood of knowledge, and has the characteristic property of boys: it can talk but cannot generate; for it is fruitful of controversy but barren of works.' Elsewhere Bacon speaks of the 'contentious and thorny philosophy of Aristotle.' Modern philosophy . . . seeks to put an end to the contentiousness of Socratic philosophy by finding a method that will at once produce agreement and truth. As far as I know, Strauss was the first, or at least the most radical, of those who have challenged this entire enterprise—in perhaps 400 years. Those who have heretofore challenged modernity—for example, Rousseau, Nietzsche, and Heidegger—have done so, either originally or in the end, on the basis of a more radical modernity. Strauss alone, so far as I know, has challenged modernity . . . from a point of view absolutely detached from its roots and its branches. . . ."

This provoked—or elicited—one further reply. I was told that I was "certainly right in saying that Leo Strauss is the most radical challenger of the entire modern enterprise." With this challenge, my correspondent declared, he had "considerable sympathy." However, he said,

> we live in modernity, not elsewhere, and I think it a simple matter of prudence to "work within the system," to the degree that we can. One of the reasons I feel that way is that all rebellions against modernity in our century seemed destined to assume monstrous shapes. Besides, I am essentially a reformist and a meliorist by temperament.

To this accordingly I responded as follows:

"There certainly is no difference between us on the proposition that we must 'live in modernity, not elsewhere,' and that it is "a simple matter of prudence to 'work within the system.'" I agree emphatically that the typical 'rebellions against modernity in our century . . . have assumed monstrous shapes.' Like you, I think of myself as 'essentially a reformist and a meliorist by temperament.' Where then do we differ?

"One must, I think, be a meliorist and reformist, not only by temperament, but by conviction. Reformism and meliorism have their proper home only within a decent system, which offers reasonable modes of redress and of change. What place is there for reformism and meliorism in a Nazi concentration camp, or in the Gulag Archipelago? The ultimate indictment of American slavery was not the brutal treatment—real or alleged—of the slaves. No matter what material rewards were offered within the system, the fact remains that however talented, industrious, and ambitious a slave might be, he could never look forward to freedom. In the generation before the Civil War, nearly all roads leading towards emancipation were systematically cut off. In the end, reform was not possible, and war became necessary.

"Strauss' indictment of the 'new political science' was above all that it abstracted from the differences between a decent and humane constitutionalism, and the vilest of tyrannies. The reductionism of such a science led to the characterization of the political phenomena in terms of the subrational, in terms of impulses, urges, drives, and desires. In the urge and drive to quantify, qualities disappeared, and the differences of regimes disappeared from the characterization of regimes.

"The rebellions against modernity which have taken such monstrous shapes have done so because they have taken the forms of radicalizations of modernity. Because his detachment from modernity was so much greater than all previous critics of modernity, Strauss alone could supply us with a theoretical foundation for a moderate politics within modernity. For Strauss *did* have a practical teaching, and it took the form of a celebration of the virtues, above all, of Anglo-American constitutionalism at its best. The preoccupation, among his students, with the American Founders, with Lincoln, and with Churchill, is a direct reflection of this teaching.

"But liberal democracy, Strauss taught, although it may treat many things unequal in themselves, as being politically equal, cannot treat the principles of liberal democracy as being no better or worse than their denial. Yet it was neutrality upon this life and death issue that constituted the heart of the 'new political science.' This is what Strauss meant when he said that the fiddlers did not even know that Rome was burning. Is it not absurd then, for the sake of meliorism and reformism, to have a fiddlers' award in the name of Leo Strauss?"

A further objection to my letter to the editor of the *American Political Science Review* took the form of a query, whether this was the proper time to remind the profession of Strauss' opinion of it. What made "this time" improper, I gathered, was the willingness of so many with whom Strauss had differed to join in expressing pious regard for his memory. Surely such piety is commendable, and one should let the dead past bury its dead. But what of the living future of political philosophy? Strauss' life was a struggle against its grave diggers. In such a case, what has piety, any more than tradition, to do with right action? Strauss frequently pointed to the absence of piety from the lists of the virtues in the *Nicomachean Ethics*. And he just as frequently pointed to the one passage in that book where piety is mentioned. It is where Aristotle, differing with the school of Plato, declares that, although both are dear to us, piety requires that we honor truth even before our friends. Certainly Socrates' piety consisted in nothing so much as his philosophizing, in the face of any threat, or any tempation whatever. Strauss' quarrel with contemporary political science resembled Socrates' quarrel with the disciples of the ancient poets. For the myths of modern science upon which the academic discipline of political science today so largely rests, are the pre-Socratic poetry of modernity. To obscure, much less to forget, this quarrel, is to obscure or to forget the purpose of Strauss' life, however one may piously intend to remember his name.

A final objection to my argument was that the Strauss Award was unlikely to have any grave consequences, either good or bad. This is perhaps the most difficult of all objections to deal with. Surely none of us who teach political philosophy—and that certainly included Strauss—expect anything we do or say (or write) to have "grave consequences," as the world usually understands these matters. All of Strauss' work took place within the setting of what he called the crisis of the West. A diagnosis and prognosis of that crisis was the expressed or implied preface to nearly all of his reading of the great books. And the deepening of his understanding of that crisis was almost invariably part of the conclusion of such reading. Yet he never seems to have thought that his work would alter the course of that crisis—except as that crisis was also a crisis within the souls of those whom he taught. Like Churchill—whom, I think, he admired more than any other man of his time—Strauss seemed to think that there are struggles which one has a duty to carry on, without regard to the prospect of success. But—again, like Churchill—he was no determinist, and did not believe that any cause is doomed to failure, simply because the odds against it are great.

Strauss was primarily concerned with the quality of human life. How does one live well? What is virtue? and What is the best regime? were alternative forms of fundamentally the same question. But good action is its own end, and the gravity of an action is to be understood primarily with respect to its excellence, and not with respect to its consequences. So it seems to me that whether or not the Strauss Award has grave consequences is less important than whether its establishment is in itself a good or bad action. My argument was directed primarily towards demonstrating that it was a bad action, whose consequences—if there were any—were also bound to be bad.

Political philosophy is concerned to know the principles of political actions, which in their true or comprehensive meaning, are the principles of human action. The teachers of political philosophy, like all other human beings, reveal the quality of their principles by deed no less than by speech. They carry a greater responsibility for their actions than other human beings, since their discipline implies that they have taken greater thought than other human beings, to know what is the human good, and hence how to act well. If they do not act well, within whatever sphere is theirs, however small, and especially if they undermine thoughtful speech by thoughtless action, they inevitably corrupt the young. Can there be any graver consequence than that?

In the tenth book of the *Nicomachean Ethics*, Aristotle says that in matters of passions and actions, words *(logoi)* are less persuasive than deeds *(erga)*. Whenever the latter are out of harmony with the former, they provoke contempt, and in addition bring destruction *(prosanairousin)* upon the truth. But when, on the contrary, words *(logoi)* are not only true, but in harmony with deeds, they persuade, and urge on towards a life in accordance with them [1172 a 35-b7]. Surely, the doctrine of this passage is ineluctably part of any serious effort to revive the study of political philosophy, in the spirit of Leo Strauss.

In the second book of the *Politics*, Aristotle takes to task one Hippodamus who, he says, was the first man, not engaged in political activity, to speak of the best regime. Among Hippodamus' proposals, was one which would honor anyone who discovered something useful for the city. Some of the profoundest sentences Strauss ever wrote are in his interpretation of Aristotle's critique of Hippodamus, in *The City and Man.* "On the basis of some observations made nearer home," Strauss wrote, for example, "one might suspect a connection between Hippodamus' unbridled concern with clarity and simplicity and his unbridled concern with technological progress." How near to home was Strauss' suspicion, perhaps not even he suspected. What could be more evident than the advantage of having something better, whether it be a mousetrap or a law? And how better to have something better, than to reward the inventor? Strauss is at some pains to expound Aristotle's account of Hippodamus' simplemindedness in his failure to understand the difference between improvement in the arts, and improvement in the laws. It is comical self-contradiction moreover, to make a proposal implying the possibility of unlimited change in what is supposed to be the best regime. Yet even supposing the desirability of change in the laws, Aristotle asks, is it proper to introduce change into all laws, or only into some? Into every regime, or not into every regime? And is anyone to introduce these changes, or only certain people? [*Politics*, 1269 a 25–28] Aristotle does not answer these latter questions here. Yet is it not clear that by proposing a contest for honor, in the city, by the city, Hippodamus is proposing what is necessarily a *political* contest? How can any such contest differ in its essential nature from any other politcal contest for honor, or for office? The reason why Hippodamus did not understand the difference between art and law, was that at bottom he did not understand the difference between philosophy and politics. It was above all because of this that he could not become the first political philosopher.

The rebirth of political philosophy, no less than its birth, depends upon comprehending the difference between politics and philosophy. The promoters of the Leo Strauss Award, by proposing to recognize political philosophy by a political process, have subordinated political philosophy to the political process. In so doing, they have shown themselves heirs of Hippodamus, not of Aristotle or of Strauss. Undertaking to promote the recognition of political philosophy, they have in fact promoted only the recognition of political skill, whether their own, or that of prospective award winners and award committees. Yet they are excused by two apparent facts: they do not recognize what it is they are *not* promoting; and because of this, they can not know what it is they *are* promoting in its place.

Endnotes

EQUALITY AS A CONSERVATIVE PRINCIPLE

1. On the difference between the Whiggery of the English and American Revolutions, see H. V. Jaffa, *Equality and Liberty: Theory and Practice in American Politics*, (New York: Oxford University Press, 1965), ch. 6 [hereinafter cited as *Equality and Liberty.*]

2. 5 *The Rambler* (New Series), May, 1861, at 17 (reprinted in *Essays on Freedom and Power* 171 [G. Himmelfarb ed. 1955]).

3. *The Contest in America* (1862). Preprinted from *Fraser's Magazine*, Feb.–May, 1862.

4. See text accompanying notes 37–38 *infra*.

5. *Basic Symbols*, p. 156.

6. H. V. Jaffa, *Crisis of the House Divided: An Interpretation of the Issues in the Lincoln–Douglas Debates* (Doubleday, 1959; Reissued in paper with a new Introduction, University of Washington Press, 1973). Hereinafter this will be cited as *Crisis*.

7. 2 A. de Tocqueville, *Democracy in America* 34–35, 99–103, 215–21, 226–27, 304–05 (H. Reeve ed. 1945).

8. 1 *The Collected Works of Abraham Lincoln* 108–15 (R. Basler ed. 1953). Hereinafter cited as *Lincoln*.

9. *Id.* at 271–79.

10. Kendall, Book Review, 7 *National Review* 461 (159). Hereinafter cited as Book Review.

11. W. Kendall, *The Conservative Affirmation* 249–52 (1963).

12. Book Review, *supra* note 10, at 461.

13. *Id.*

14. *Id.*

15. *Id.* at 461–62.

16. *Id.*

17. In 100 *Years of Emancipation* 1 (R. Goldwin ed. 1963). Reprinted in *Equality and Liberty*, *supra* note 1, at 140.

18. Book Review, *supra* note 10, at 462.

19. *Id.*

20. *Id.*

21. Dred Scott v. Sanford, 60 U.S. (19 How.) 393 (1857).

22. Book Review, *supra* note 10, at 462.

23. 4 *Lincoln*, *supra* note 8, at 263.

24. See note 17 *supra* and accompanying text.

25. Book Review, *supra* note 10, at 462.

26. Dred Scot v. Stanford, 60 U.S. (19 How.) (1857).

27. Book Review, *supra* note 10, at 461–62.

28. *4 Lincoln, supra* note 8, at 270 (footnotes omitted).

29. Book Review, *supra note* 10, at 461–62.

30. *Id.* at 462.

31. *Id.*

32. *Id.*

33. *2 Lincoln, supra* note 8, at 520.

34. *4 Lincoln, supra* note 8, at 438.

35. Pp. 14, 156.

36. Pp. 14–15 (emphasis added).

37. *Sources of Our Liberties* 311–82 (R. Perry ed. 1964).

38. *Id.* at 346.

39. J. Locke, *Two Treatises of Government* 7 (T. Cook ed. 1947). Hereinafter cited as *Two Treatises*.

40. *Documents of American History* 92 (H. Cammager ed. 1963). Hereinafter cited as *Documents*.

41. *Two Treatises, supra* note 39, at 8.

42. *Id.*

43. *History of Political Philosophy* 451 (L. Strauss and J. Cropsey eds. 1972).

44. *Id.*

45. *Id.*

46. *Two Treatises, supra* note 39, at 121.

47. *Id.*

48. *Id.*

49. *2 Lincoln, supra* note 8, at 266.

50. *The Federalist* 337 (Modern Library ed. 1937). Hereinafter cites as *The Federalist*.

51. *2 Lincoln, supra* note 8, at 266.

52. *Id.* at 499.

53. *The Federalist, supra* note 50, at 55 (emphasis added).

54. *7 Lincoln, supra* note 8, at 259–60.

55. Pp. 88, 90.

56. *4 Lincoln, supra* note 8, at 433 (footnotes omitted).

57. *Documents, supra* note 40, at 100 (editor's note).

58. *A Casebook on the Declaration of Independence* 32 (R. Ginsberg ed. 1967).

59. *4 Letters and Other Writings of James Madison* 392 (R. Worthington ed. 1884).

60. *Id.* at 391.

61. *Id.*

62. *Id.* at 392.

HOW TO THINK ABOUT THE AMERICAN REVOLUTION

1. *America's Continuing Revolution*, (Garden City, N.Y.: Anchor/Doubleday, 1976). This title will henceforward be abbreviated, in these notes, as *ACR*. The engrossed text of the Declaration of Independence is so familiar to an American audience, and is available in so many places, that no separate annotations will be made to citations of it.

2. See: "Fragment on the Constitution and the Union," in *The Collected Works of Abraham Lincoln*, Roy P. Basler, ed., (New Brunswick, New Jersey: Rutgers University Press, 1953), Vol IV, p. 168. This title will henceforward be referred to as *Collected Works*. For a commentary on this notable passage in Lincoln's writings, see: *Crisis of the House Divided*, (Seattle: University of Washington Press, 1973), pp. 330–333.

3. *ACR*, p. 9.

4. Ibid., p. 8.

5. Ibid., pp. 8, 9.

6. Ibid., p. 9.

7. Ibid., p. 21.

8. Ibid., p. 7.

9. *Documents of American History*, Henry Steele Commager, ed., (New York: Appleton-Century-Crofts, Seventh Edition, 1963), Vol. I, p. 329.

10. Harper & Row. New York & London, 1965.

11. *ACR*, p. 11.

12. Ibid., p. 11, 12.

13. Ibid., p. 12.

14. *The Federalist*, Modern Library Edition, p. 287.

15. *Letters & Other Writings of James Madison*, R. Worthington, ed., (1884), Vol. IV, p. 392.

16. *ACR*, p. 13.

17. *The Papers of Alexander Hamilton*, (New York: Columbia University Press 1961), Vol. I, p. 122.

18. *ACR*, pp. 4, 5.

19. *Collected Works*, III, 376.

20. *The Writings of Thomas Jefferson*, Paul Leicester Ford, ed., (New York: Putnam, 1892–1899), Vol. X, p. 391. This title, where evident, will be referred to as *Writings*.

21. *Collected Works*, IV, 240.

22. Ibid., I, 438.

23. Op. cit., p. 3.

24. *Collected Works*, III, p. 522.

25. *Writings*, I, p. 440.

26. Ibid., II, p. 52.

27. Ibid., III, pp. 266, 267.

28. Ibid., p. 267.

29. Ibid.

30. *Collected Works*, VIII, p. 333.

31. *Writings*, III, p. 267.

32. Ibid., IV, p. 185.

33. Ibid., X, p. 157.

34. *Collected Works*, IV, pp. 432, 433.

35. *The Conditions of Freedom*, (Baltimore: The Johns Hopkins Press, 1975), Chapter 8.

36. Op. cit., p. 341.

37. *The Writings of James Madison*, Gaillard Hunt, ed., (New York: Putnam, 1910), Vol. X, *ad finem*. Facsimile in the handwriting of Mrs. Madison.

38. *ACR*, p. 2.
39. Ibid., p. 11.
40. Ibid., p. 12.
41. Ibid.
42. *The American Revolution*, 1775–1783, John Richard Alden, (New York: Harper & Brothers, 1954), p. 76. In a footnote on the previous page, Alden writes as follows: "Early in January [1776] Washington commented bitterly on the King's Speech. On January 31 he referred to 'the sound doctrine and unanswerable reasoning' of Tom Paine's *Common Sense*." Professor Kristol, be it noted, complains that we do not sufficiently attend to the wisdom of George Washington, while asking us to ignore the man whose reasoning on independence Washington called unanswerable.
43. Ibid., p. 77.
44. *The Life & Works of Thomas Paine*, (New Rochelle, N.Y.: The Thomas Paine Association, 1924, Patriots Edition), Vol. II, p. 263.
45. *Collected Works*, II, p. 407.
46. *Writings*, III, p. 263.
47. *ACR*, p. 26.
48. Ibid., p. 25.
49. Ibid., p. 27.
50. Ibid., p. 30.
51. Ibid.
52. Ibid.
53. *Time on the Cross* (Boston: Little Brown & Company, 1974), Vol. I, The Economics of American Negro Slavery, p. 24.
54. The text of the Northwest Ordinance, from which we have taken the foregoing excerpts, is to be found in Commager's *Documents*, cited in note 9 above, Vol. I, pp. 128–132.
55. *Writings*, IX, p. 276.
56. *ACR*, p. 38.
57. *The Basic Symbols of the American Political Tradition*, Willmoore Kendall and George Carey, (Baton Rouge: Louisiana State University Press, 1970), p. 83. Emphasis has been added to the original.
58. *The Works of John C. Calhoun*, Richard Cralle, ed., (New York: Appleton, 1854), Vol. 4, p. 507.
59. Ibid., p. 508. Emphasis added.
60. *Collected Works*, II, p. 532.
61. *ACR*, pp. 25, 26.
62. *Collected Works*, III, p. 27. But consider also the following. "Now, let the people of the free-states adopt these sentiments. . . ." "What! Do you mean to say that anything in these sentiments requires us to believe it. . . ." "If it be insisted that men may support Douglas's measures, without adopting his sentiments, let it be tested. . . ." Ibid., p. 430.
63. Ibid., II, p. 385.
64. Ibid., III, pp. 441, 442. But consider also, "Public opinion in this country is everything." Ibid., III, p. 424.
65. Ibid., VII, p. 271.
66. Ibid., II, p. 256.

67. Ibid., p. 264.

68. Ibid., IV, pp. 253, 254.

69. Commager, *Documents*, Vol. I, p. 342.

70. *ACR*, p. 26.

71. It is a matter of the greatest regret that Professor Diamond should have died before the publication of these lines. It is however fair to note that the mimeographed version of this essay, prepared for the annual meetings of the American Political Science Association in 1975, was distributed nearly two years before his death. Professor Diamond received a copy in the first mailing, and was invited to attend the panel at which the paper was discussed—which he declined to do. The present version, as it bears upon the question of Professor Diamond's scholarship differs in no respect from the one that was in his hands. So far as we know, he never commented upon the discrepancy between his account of the Madison-Jefferson correspondence, and the actual correspondence.

72. *ACR*, pp. 26, 27.

73. *The Writings of James Madison*, p. 218.

74. See for example: Merrill D. Peterson, in *Thomas Jefferson and the New Nation*, (Oxford: Oxford University Press, 1970), p. 986.

75. *The Writings of Thomas Jefferson*, H.A. Washington, ed., (Washington, D.C.: Taylor & Maury, 1853), Vol. VII, p. 397. According to the Editor, the address of this letter is lost. It seems on internal evidence to be the letter that was sent either to Cabell or Madison or both.

76. *Writings* (Ford, ed.), X, p. 189.

77. Ibid., p. 376.

78. *Letters and Other Writings of James Madison* (Worthington, ed.), Vol. III, p. 483.

79. *The Writings of James Madison* (Hunt, ed.) IX, p. 218, 219.

80. See his: "What the Framers Meant by Federalism," in *A Nation of States*, (Chicago: Rand McNally, 1974, Second Edition).

81. *The Writings of James Madison* (Hunt, ed.), IX, p. 219.

82. Consider the discussion of express and implied powers in *Federalist #44*, of which Madison was the author. It is difficult to say which of the doctrines of construction later identified with Hamilton and Marshall are not anticipated and patronized here by Madison. How in the world they escaped the notice of Jefferson is a mystery.

83. Op. cit., p. 219. The places that the *Federalist* had "actually been admitted" is something of a tacit confession of its imperfect respectability. Jefferson had remarked that Rhode Island, being the most commerical of the states, was also the one most lacking in virtue!

84. Ibid., pp. 219, 220.

85. Ibid., p. 220.

86. Ibid.

87. Ibid.

88. Ibid., p. 221.

89. *The Writings of Thomas Jefferson*, Andrew A. Lipscomb, Editor-in-Chief, Albert Ellery Bergh, Managing Editor, (Washington, D.C.: The Thomas Jefferson Memorial Association, 1903), Vol. XIX, pp. 460, 461. This meeting of the Board of Visitors was held on March 4, 1825, twenty-four days after Madison had written his letter recommending the "text and documents" which were to be used in the

school. The meeting was attended by Jefferson, as Rector of the University, and by Madison, George Loyall, John H. Cocke, and Joseph C. Cabell, as members of the Board.

90. *ACR*, pp. 27, 28.

91. *Writings* (Ford, ed.), X, p. 391.

92. *ACR*, p. 28.

93. *The Works of John Locke*, (London: 1824), Vol. 4, pp. 339, 340. [Chapter 2, paragraph 4 of the *Second Treatise*].

94. See note 14 above.

95. Compare Leo Strauss: ". . . Locke sees the crucially important consequence of the natural right of self-preservation in the natural right of property, *i.e.*, of acquiring property. . . ." Article on "Natural Law" in *International Encyclopedia of the Social Sciences*, David Sills, ed, (The Macmillan Company & The Free Press: 1968), Vol. 11, p. 84.

96. For a parallel discussion of this theme, see my discussion in article on "Natural Rights." Op. cit. (note 95), Vol. 11, pp. 85–89.

97. *ACR*, pp. 29, 30.

98. *The Writings of George Washington*, collected and edited by Worthington Chauncey Ford, (New York & London: Putname's, 1891), Vol. X, p. 265.

99. Op. cit., p. 243.

100. Ibid., p. 80.

101. *Writings* (Ford, ed.), I, p. 429.

102. Ibid., V, p. 147.

103. Ibid., X, p. 42.

104. *ACR*, p. 29.

105. *The Democratic Republic: An Introduction to American National Government*, Martin Diamond, Winston Mills Fisk, & Herbert Garfinkel, (Chicago: Rand McNally & Company, Second Edition, 1970). Chapters 1–5, 9, and 16 are by Professor Diamond, according to the Preface. Our quotation is from p. 4 (of Chapter I).

106. *ACR*, p. 231.

107. Ibid. The quotation from Professor Mansfield is from his essay, "Thomas Jefferson," in *American Political Thought*, Morton J. Frisch and Richard G. Stevens, eds., (New York: Charles Scribner's Sons, 1971), pp. 38, 39.

108. *Writings* (Ford, ed.), I, p. 447.

109. *ACR*, pp. 36, 37.

110. *Writings* (Ford, ed.), X, p. 38.

111. *Collected Works*, II, p. 266.

112. Ibid., III, p. 375.

113. In "Prefatory Note" to *The "Higher Law" Background of American Constitutional Law*, Edward S. Corwin, (Great Seals Books, Cornell University Press, 1955), p. v.

114. Op. cit., p. 1.

115. Ibid., pp. 1, 2.

116. Commager, *Documents*, I, p. 187. For some strange reason, the Ford Edition of Jefferson's *Writings* does not give the printed text of his first inaugural address.

117. See also: "What Is Equality? The Declaration of Independence Revisited," Chapter 8 of *The Conditions of Freedom* (*supra*, note 35). In note 2, p. 153, I

observed that this correspondence of the three persons of God with the three powers of government was first marked by Professor George Anastaplo, in his "The Declaration of Independence," *St. Louis University Law Journal*, Vol. 9 (1965), p. 390.

118. *Collected Works*, III, p. 550.

119. In 1789 Jefferson had declared to Madison that "an apostasy from Republicanism to royalism is unprecedented and impossible." *Writings* (Ford, ed.), V, p. 83. Yet today the most tyrannical regimes ever seen on the face of the earth call themselves "peoples democracies."

120. *American Historical Review*, Vol. XXX, No. 3 (April, 1925), pp. 451–477.

121. *Politics* 1281 a 15–21. Translated by HVJ. Many translators of this passage omit the oath by the democrats, substituting some present-day colloquial indication of emphasis. So far as I know, this is the only oath in the *Politics*, certainly it is the only oath taken in the name of Zeus. That Aristotle took this occasion to indicate the most emphatic form of political speech—the occasion when a democratic argument is supported by an appeal to the highest of Olympian deities to justify the extreme of injustice—is certainly itself significant in the highest degree.

122. *Federalist* #48. Op. cit., pp. 324, 325. Compare the same passage in *Writings* (Ford, ed.), III, pp. 223, 224.

123. See note 2, above.

EQUALITY, JUSTICE, AND THE AMERICAN REVOLUTION

1. "The Heresy of Equality," op. cit., p. 62.
2. Modern Library Edition, p. 340.
3. 1131 a 10 to 1131 b 24.
4. 1301 b 27.
5. Modern Library Edition, p. 3.
6. "The Heresy of Equality," op. cit., p. 63.
7. "It was not because it was proposed to establish a new nation, but because it was proposed to establish a nation on new principles, that July 4, 1776, has come to be regarded as one of the greatest days in history." And again. "But we should search these charters [of the Dutch and of the British] in vain for an assertion of the doctrine of equality. This principle had not before appeared as an official political declaration of any nation. It was profoundly revolutionary. It is one of the corner stones of American institutions." President Calvin Coolidge, speaking on the one hundred and fiftieth anniversary of the Declaration of Independence. In *Foundations of the Republic: Speeches and Addresses* by Calvin Coolidge (New York and London: Scribner's, 1926), pp. 445, 447.
8. "The Heresy of Equality," op. cit., p. 62.
9. Ibid., p. 66.
10. *The Works of John C. Calhoun*, Richard K. Cralle, ed., (New York: Appleton, 1854), Vol. 4, p. 507.
11. Ibid.
12. Ibid., p. 508.
13. *Documents of American History*, Henry Steele Commager, ed., (New York: Appleton-Century-Crofts, Seventh Edition, 1963), pp. 97, 98.

Endnotes

14. *The Collected Works of Abraham Lincoln*, Roy P. Basler, ed., (New Brunswick, New Jersey: Rutgers University Press, 1953), Vol. 2, pp. 398–410.

15. Calhoun, op. cit., pp. 505, 506.

16. "The Heresy of Equality," op. cit., p. 67.

17. Ibid., pp. 67, 68.

18. Commager, op. cit., p. 107.

19. Ibid.

20. Ibid., p. 103.

21. Calhoun, op. cit., p. 512

22. Bradford, "The Heresy of Equality," op. cit., p. 77 (note 36.)

23. Ibid., pp. 70, 71.

24. Ibid., p. 71.

25. *Collected Works*, Vol. 4, p. 160.

26. *The Political History of the Great Rebellion*, Edward McPherson, ed., (Washington, D.C. 1865), p. 103.

27. Ibid.

28. Ibid.

29. Ibid., p. 104.

30. Ibid.

31. E.g. in "On the Nature of Civil and Religious Liberty," *Equality and Liberty* (Oxford, 1965), pp. 169–189.

090756